THE
GLOBAL
MARKETPLACE

THE
GLOBAL
MARKETPLACE

Edited by
Jerome M. Rosow
President, Work in America Institute, Inc., USA

Facts On File
New York • Oxford

The Global Marketplace

Library of Congress Cataloging-in-Publication Data

The Global marketplace / edited by Jerome M. Rosow.
    p. cm.
  Includes index.
  ISBN 0-8160-1633-X
  1. Competition, International. 2. International economic
relations. 3. International finance. I. Rosow, Jerome M.
HF1414.G56 1988
338.8'8—dc19   88-16279

British CIP data available on request

Printed in the United States of America

10 9 8 7 6 5 4 3 2 1

CONTENTS

ACKNOWLEDGMENTS

This book would not have been completed without the commitment of Carol Nardi, my executive assistant. She handled many of the contacts with the contributing authors and all of the follow-through with their respective staff. Her persistence and thoroughness assured that the contributions were coordinated and received within the publication deadline.

Beatrice Walfish assisted me in editing and organizing the Overview chapter and provided invaluable assistance.

Kate Kelly, my editor at Facts On File, always makes a strong personal commitment to each book and this book in particular. Her editorial skills and enthusiasm are reflected in the final product.

To Rosalyn, my wife, and to my sons, Michael and Joel.

THE
GLOBAL
MARKETPLACE

THE GLOBAL MARKETPLACE— AN OVERVIEW

Jerome M. Rosow
President
Work in America Institute, Inc., USA

The one interdependent world espoused by presidential nominee Wendell Willkie in 1940 is closer to fruition than ever before with the emergence in the 1980s of a "global marketplace." In such an economy, competition transcends national boundaries, driven by increasingly sophisticated channels of communication, the instantaneous transmittal of information on a worldwide basis, and by new and faster methods of capital transfer. The forces of change have altered the face of the economy, calling for new attitudes on the part of business, a retreat from nationalism, and practical responses to a marketplace that demands world-class products.

How business responds to these forces is the theme of this collection of essays by the chief executives of ten major multinational companies, based on their experiences in the global marketplace. Each chapter is written from a very special perspective—that of the CEO of a company that occupies a predominant position within its own industry. Each writer describes candidly the corporate culture of his company and the constraints within which it operates; he defines the critical issues that will determine the company's ability to survive in

1

the tough, competitive marketplace; and he describes what he sees as the company's role in the global economy of the 1990s.

The individual chapters are as unique as the companies that they describe, but, together, they provide a composite of the strategic concepts and business plans currently espoused by multinationals today. Seven themes appear in one or more chapters—occasionally in all—and serve to define the relevant issues.

- Decentralization to national or regional markets
- Creation of joint ventures with foreign partners
- Efforts to increase employee commitment
- Competition in the global capital market
- Localization of production and marketing
- Production of world-class products of the highest quality
- Investment in research, development, and technology

These themes are not mutually exclusive. Often they overlap and reinforce each other. All are significant and interrelated.

DECENTRALIZATION TO NATIONAL OR REGIONAL MARKETS

The corporate response to a world marketplace requires an organizational change, namely, the reshaping of the corporation to serve multiple markets and to compete at all levels—cost, quality, and service—in all countries. The change generally takes the form of decentralization to overseas operations, even though the classic preference of corporations has always been for centralized authority. The shift from a home or national identity to a multinational identity differs from company to company, in accordance with corporate history, age, experience, and the adaptability of the leadership to customs and practices throughout the world, but it nearly always requires decentralization.

When decentralization takes place, delegation of authority and responsibility are inevitable—and even preferable. Corporate staffs at the top are restructured, downsized, and realigned to streamline decisions, while the operational aspects of production and marketing usually directed from the center are delegated to profit centers and/or to individual countries or geographical areas.

The multiplicity of investments in many different countries—as well as the trade policies of individual localities—requires an organization system that blends well with the local environmental business climate. Decentralized management, with a predominance of nationals in management and with increased reliance upon decisions made in "the field," has been tried and tested as the long-term solution to this problem—and has succeeded. Increased reliance upon decentralized management instead of on headquarters is a clear recognition of the maturation of managerial trust and the management development process.

JOINT VENTURES, OR INTERNATIONAL PARTNERSHIPS

The development of joint ventures, or international partnerships, is the new reality in a global marketplace, reflecting the inevitable lowering of trade barriers and the opening of sheltered markets to freer competition. The sanctity of national markets, such as that of the United States, is being eroded by the forces of competition and the need to control inflation.

Joint ventures, in the context of this book, are simply partnerships between two or more corporations based in two or more home countries. These partnerships may involve shared investments and differing degrees of managerial participation in operations. They are akin to acquisitions (but at only a fraction of the cost) in that the partners acquire a share of each other's competitive advantages—without the long lead time and higher investment costs of solo development.

The most exciting and far-reaching implications of multinational joint ventures are still on the horizon. One implication is their truly global character, as opposed to the rather narrow considerations that necessarily color the competition between industries in individual home countries. American competitiveness, for example, implies a deep concern for the U.S. trade balance and the U.S. share of its own market versus foreign imports. In a global context, competitiveness translates into the ability of American corporations to vie for worldwide markets with multinational corporations in other countries. Thus, American corporations must think, plan, and invest in international competitive systems that can simultaneously penetrate and sustain sales in a multiplicity of foreign markets as well as in the domestic market. The geographical scope of the market is the entire world.

A global economy also means that the corporations of a single country, say, the United States, may export to many markets, produce and sell in others, and retain or increase market share at home in the domestic market. This is a delicate balancing act, which thrives upon free trade abroad and struggles with free trade at home. Joint ventures are a key element in this global strategy.

Once corporate planning has become global, the issue of solo management versus joint investments becomes more crucial to the future of the enterprise. The fact that the contributors to this book are actively engaged in cross-national or multinational joint ventures is more than a harbinger of the future scenario, it is the future. The elusive "one world" of the 1940s may become an economic reality as these combinations of massive corporate wealth, technology, and personnel create new forces for innovation and new partnerships in world trade. These cooperative ventures should increase the efficiency of industries and business while also leading to increased understanding and cooperation. They should also reduce nationalism, ethnocentrism, and xenophobia—all of which pose a threat to the global market.

In recent years, the number and variety of joint ventures have validated their popularity and their permanent place in a global economy. Roger Smith of General Motors describes a typical joint venture with his account of the creation of a world-class car in a multinational setting, embracing partners from four different countries—Korea, the United States, Ireland, and West Germany. James Olson of AT&T describes the efforts of one of the biggest and most resourceful corporations in the world in reaching out to the global marketplace through its new role in international telecommunications. In the current economic climate, competitive advantage has become more fragile and more transitory. Alliances, on the other hand, are driven by practical realities and the sure knowledge that there is strength in such alliances that transcends the single enterprise—especially since alliances generally combine business skills that are complementary and often synergetic.

The implications of multinational joint ventures are profound. While the contributors to this book describe their own experiences candidly, they do not always examine the adjustments required to develop and sustain the teamwork, trust, and cooperation called for by a successful cross-national partnership. In a world economy, these partnerships must succeed, but they will continue to require considerable staying power and mutual trust, since the partners in one venture are often competitors in other ventures. The pay-offs, however, are enormous—profits, growth, and an improved standard of living for people everywhere.

EFFORTS TO INCREASE EMPLOYEE COMMITMENT

The cutting edge of world competition has exposed every multinational corporation to external forces that penetrate to the very core of management. Cost pressures, differing competitive advantages, rising customer expectations, the mobility of capital, and the pressure to sustain market share have shaken the corporate world. Responding to an unstable world economy and to the surge of competition, corporate leadership has become much more aware of the value of human resources and the importance of increasing employee commitment.

Capital and technology are essential in manufacturing a quality product, but human efforts multiply their value. Corporations are becoming increasingly aware of this truth and are striving to elevate the human side of their enterprise. They recognize that the motivation and involvement of the corporate work force at all levels, from shop floor to executive suite, is critical to the achievement of cost control, productivity, product quality, customer service, and market share. Based upon trust, involvement, and employment security, employee commitment acts as a catalyst for change and sustains a competitive edge for the company.

Anders Lindström of the Carnegie Group, in Sweden, highlights the increased need for employee commitment as the basis for effective management. He recognizes the significance of employee participation in decision making to sustain a change-oriented environment at work. Participation, he says, requires open channels of communication on basic company objectives and operations, a continuing dialogue with employees, and increased attention to gains sharing in terms of ownership and/or profit sharing or other financial incentives.

General Motors' Roger Smith emphasizes the necessity for solid partnerships between management and employees in order to achieve the effective application of technology. He considers the strengthening of human resources as the first order of business in GM's blueprint for the future. Smith is seeking a change in the corporate culture of this giant enterprise, with the goal of better decisions and greater participation by employees at every level. He believes that partnerships between employees, based on the team concept, and a shift from adversarial to cooperative employee and union relationships with management, hold the key to the delivery of the best product to customers at a price they can afford, while providing a satisfactory profit to the business.

GLOBAL CAPITAL MARKETS

The world of finance is experiencing a period of extraordinary change, accelerated by the information revolution. A global capital marketplace has emerged, which contributes to the rapid transnational movement of capital and which is fundamental to economic development, a higher standard of living, and a better balance of wealth among the nations of the world.

The global capital marketplace, a relatively new phenomenon in international business, trade, and investment, has stimulated and will continue to stimulate world competition for capital, which is uninhibited by long-term planning cycles, and seeks the highest level of return. Thus, competition in the global marketplace depends on successfully gaining and retaining large capital sums to finance and support the competitive position of each nation. Each enterprise is a player in this high-risk, high-stakes world game.

Speaking from his vantage point as chairman and CEO of PaineWebber, Donald Marron traces the development of the global marketplace and identifies four separate factors that have contributed to this development: globalization, deregulation, computerization, and securitization. He defines globalization as the tendency of capital to ignore national boundaries in the quest for maximum return; deregulation as the dismantling of rules and restrictions, creating both opportunity and turmoil; computerization as the expanding role of electronic systems and their function in supporting and accelerating decisions; and securitization as the tendency of capital to be treated as a commodity in its own right.

Deregulation, as viewed against the background of the October 19, 1987, stock market collapse, could have a major effect on long-term safety and security in the United States, Japan, the United Kingdom, and Germany. Moreover, deregulation has created the need for self-regulation by national institutions and industrial firms and will certainly lead to a reassessment of deregulation versus controls in the interest of international financial stability.

LOCALIZATION UNDER "PREVAILING NATIONAL PRACTICES"

Generally, multinational corporations that seek overseas markets have been drawn into locally based manufacturing. This is a response to governmental policies and realistic concern over trade barriers, which restrict market access. Today, the massive investment of Japan in U.S. industry and business ($3.9 billion in 1987) is viewed as confirmation of the long-term necessity to produce within the country that consumes the product. German, Dutch, Swedish, British, and other multinationals are also investing in the United States, or forming joint ventures here and in other countries.

Investments abroad have expanded enormously since 1950, and foreign investments in the United States have grown even faster. Thus, one of the most obvious responses to the global marketplace has been a physical presence within the individual, national marketplace. The export mercantile world of the past is shrinking, and home-country-based production and marketing are beginning to predominate.

Edmund Pratt of Pfizer notes with obvious pride that minimal presence of expatriates in Pfizer's worldwide operations. Sekimoto of NEC confirms this viewpoint and attests to the importance of nation-based investments, conforming to local prevailing practice and managed by national executives who are an integral part of that society.

"When in Rome do as the Romans do!" is emerging as the most effective corporate policy. This philosophy is consistent with decentralization and seeks to overcome the barriers of nationalistic differences by coopting national values and conforming to local customs and practices. Local management also increases the corporation's ability to melt into the national business landscape and to relate products and marketing to local preferences.

Localization is also more responsive to a customer-driven strategy because it can more easily tailor its products and its marketing to national tastes and customs. The difference between export competition and national on-site production is illustrated by the practices of many of the contributors, who are virtually unanimous in the need for, and importance of, localization.

The global marketplace requires that multinational corporations become "corporate citizens" of the nations within which they operate. This implies a knowledge of international relations, foreign affairs, political science, government relations, and history. It requires also top management that is aware of the nation-state and its people as distinctive entities, and executives who can function as world citizens, free of prejudice and sensitive to the diversity of social, economic, and political forces affecting the business environment. "No man is an island," and no multinational company can survive within a self-centered shell of home-country values.

PRODUCTION OF WORLD-CLASS PRODUCTS

The intensification of world competition has become a battle to attract customers and to retain a significant market share over a sustained period of time. Product quality is the secret ingredient that makes it possible to produce and sell world-class products while controlling costs and sustaining competitive prices.

The concept of a world-class product is directly related to the development of an international economy, in which consumers worldwide seek the same goods and services, and in which styles cross international boundaries at a rapid rate. Products must appeal to a universal taste and, at the same time, respond to a diversity of national tastes. This task requires a flexible manufacturing and marketing posture, linked directly to marketing information sensitive to the needs of each country.

World-class global marketing translates into high-quality performance, reliability, and dependability. General Motors' Roger Smith describes the goal of "building the best" as a critical element in the company's blueprint to beat the competition in the cost versus quality war. The attainment of zero defect standards—perfect quality—is now commonly sought in the auto industry, although not always attained.

Unwavering commitment to quality is imperative at every level of the organization. Improvements in cost and quality derive not only from improved engineering and assembly, new plant design, and the effective integration of facilities, but also from new working relationships in the plant, where employee commitment is a determinant. Inconsistent quality standards are reflected in warranty losses, scrap, the high cost of quality control, and engineering costs. More than that, they are reflected in the response of the consumer. The finest marketing strategy will fail, if quality fades. A commitment to quality is difficult to sustain in the face of production pressure, but the short-term sacrifice of quality on the altar of quick profits will surely boomerang.

Above all, poor quality translates into lost sales and loss of market share, where the cost of recovery may be beyond the reach of the loser. Those who understand the meaning of quality, reliability, and performance to the customer will continue to produce world-class products; those who sacrifice quality to avoid paying investment costs or to gain immediate market advantage are destined to fail. Quality is the acid test for a world-class reputation.

RESEARCH, DEVELOPMENT, AND TECHNOLOGY

For both national and multinational corporations, technology is a critical factor in the race to maintain a competitive edge.

First and foremost is the accelerating rate of change in telecommunications, computers, and flexible manufacturing that forces organizations to adjust to rapid shifts in hardware, software, and communications and to rapid and radical changes in products and in customer demands.

Second, technology requires a direct application to the production and services generated by the business. It is critical to productivity, to costs, and to competitive pricing, and best used in combination with the effective management of human resources.

Third, technology is expensive to procure, but much more expensive to invent. The high cost of technology and the rapid rate of obsolescence imposes a constant demand for investment and mandates a responsive research and development program. For capital goods producers, in particular, the investments are enormous and lead to increased interest in joint ventures.

Finally, technological advantage is short-lived as a sustaining edge over competition. Technology transfer is an international game with rich markets and hungry competitors. Thus, there is a critical need for constant renewal, long-term plans, and sharp attention to the "technological factor" as an inherent part of global strategy. In fact, the domestic market is often the arena in which technological advantage first becomes apparent. Thus, technology is in the first line of defense in retaining the home market share as well as in penetrating new markets abroad.

The high cost of research and development and the speed of technological change have complicated the problem of competing in a world marketplace. Since no corporation and no country holds a monopoly on research and development, innovation and invention, new products, patents, licenses, and copyrights blossom throughout the free world at what seems, at times, like an alarming rate of speed.

The steady intensification of technological competition has led to much shorter innovative cycles. For example, Karlheinz Kaske of Siemens notes that 10 or 15 years used to elapse before old products were replaced by new ones; today, it takes only four or five years for obsolescence to set in. Enormous capital expenditures are required to keep up with this rate of speed, particularly in the capital goods industries. Thus, the size of the enterprise and the resources it can devote to research and development become critical factors in the race for global markets. Only a handful of companies have the resources necessary to prevail in this competition.

One means of coping with these costs is to establish partnerships—joint ventures, spanning national boundaries, which pool resources and ease the transfer and sharing of capital resources, research, managerial know-how, product design and development, marketing, and international skills. In fact, the costs of new product development and the complexity of technology may push the creation of new products far beyond the reach of the single national company and confer special competitive advantage on the largest and richest of the multinationals—or those farsighted enough to combine forces with others.

In one sense, the global marketplace is too big, too diverse, and too complex to define and analyze in one volume of essays. This collected work can, however, provide valuable insights into a significant cross-section of the world of international business competition. The chapters are independent of one another, within a common theme, and written by corporate CEOs from different national and business perspectives. The authors represent primarily U.S.-based corporations, but they are joined by contributors from Japan, Sweden, and West Germany. The organizations they represent are multinational, have been in business a long time, and are usually prominent in their industries, which include telecommunications, computers, information systems, chemicals, pharmaceuticals, banking and finance, capital goods manufacturing, consumer goods, and aluminum.

It is significant to note that the authors tend to reinforce one another in many areas—including corporate philosophy, business goals, and future objectives. All of them accept intense and increased world competition as a fact of life, focus their attention on the future, and assume direct responsibility for the outcome. They are realistic, pragmatic, and keenly aware of the new forces that have been unleashed by the information age.

Following are brief summaries of the chapters that follow.

GLOBAL COMPETITION— A STRATEGY FOR SUCCESS (Roger B. Smith)

Speaking from his perspective at the helm of the giant General Motors Corporation, Roger Smith describes how his company, severely buffeted by world competition, is meeting this challenge. He believes that all three sectors—business, labor, and government—have critical roles to play. Business must make painful adjustments, government must provide a favorable climate, and labor must assume a cooperative stance.

As one key indicator of economic interdependence, he notes that world trade has been growing about 70 percent faster than the growth rate of GNP. The U.S. auto industry, which provides a livelihood for about one in every six American workers, plays a critical economic role, he says. He describes the internationalization of competition in terms of the TRIAD nations—North America, Japan, and Europe—which account for more than 600 million people, only 15 percent of the world's population but the producer of 75 percent of the free world's products. General Motors itself employs roughly 800,000 people, working in 38 countries. Almost every part of this enterprise has been touched by technology and intensified competition.

Smith describes a strategic plan to improve GM's competitive position in four major ways: strengthening human resources, expanding technological expertise through new business acquisitions and mergers in related key industries, achieving world-class cost and quality in manufacturing, and developing new marketing strategies.

General Motors is seeking to change its entire corporate culture, to move a giant worldwide organization toward a more flexible, decentralized management. Its objective: to achieve better decisions and greater participation by employees at every level. Smith believes that Americans can no longer afford the luxury of an excessively adversarial society, and seeks, instead, a combination of the Japanese cooperative spirit with American creativity to achieve the best of both worlds.

This synthesis of ideas is also reflected in GM's second objective, its aggressive acquisitions and mergers program. The two key acquisitions are Electronic Data Systems and Hughes Aircraft, which were part of a blueprint to create a telecommunications network with GM and to accelerate the application of electronics in GM products. These acquisitions are designed to help GM speed decision making, cut costs, improve product quality, and react more quickly to a changing marketplace.

Since 1971, General Motors has entered into nearly 40 joint ventures. Two of the most important are the partnership with Toyota, in Fremont, California, and, more recently, a joint venture with the South Korean automaker Daewoo. Smith describes the latter as a truly international project, with GM's Adam Opel unit in Germany designing the car, the South Koreans building it, and the Americans and Koreans selling it. He clearly believes that joint ventures are critical to survival in the global marketplace.

The battle for cost savings and quality is the third plank in the GM strategy. Smith defines cost to include warranty, quality control, engineering, scrap and, most important, lost sales due to poor quality. He illustrates GM's conception of state-of-the-art quality with a description of the Saturn Corporation's production of an entirely new American car by an entirely new method, through "simultaneous engineering."

GM's fourth objective is its development of a new marketing strategy, which seeks to make General Motors the most market-driven, consumer-oriented company in the industry.

Smith describes the corporate reorganization of 1984, which reshaped GM's six car divisions to respond to market demands. These divisions seek to reduce the number of models, increase market penetration, and decrease overlaps among the models, resulting in a clearer image of each division. The bottom line, Smith believes, is the customer.

THE GLOBALIZATION OF CAPITAL
(Donald B. Marron)

Speaking as chairman and CEO of PaineWebber, Donald Marron discusses the emergence of the global capital marketplace and its implications. Marron believes that the global market for the buying and selling of financial services and for the rapid transnational movement of capital has increased the opportunities for economic development, a worldwide higher standard of living, and a greater balance of wealth between today's haves and have-nots.

This chapter deals with a world in which hundreds of billions of dollars are moved through the international financial markets every day at enormous speed, reflecting the internationalization of global markets in financial transactions. U.S. brokerage firms, for example, now have more than 250 branches in 32 foreign countries, and more than 110 foreign investment firms have locations in the United States.

Marron traces the development of the global capital market and identifies four inseparable factors: (1) *globalization* itself, the tendency of capital to ignore national boundaries in the quest for maximum return; (2) *deregulation*, the dismantling of rules and restrictions, creating both opportunity and turmoil; (3) *computerization*, the expanding role of electronic systems and their function in supporting and accelerating decisions; and (4) *securitization*, the tendency for capital to be treated as a commodity in its own right.

From his vantage point, Marron presents a brief history of the global capital market since the Bretton Woods Conference in 1944, including a discussion of the burgeoning Eurodollar market, the Interest Equalization Tax (IET) of 1963, the Credit Restraint Program of 1965, the abolition of exchange controls in 1971, the creation of floating currency exchange rates, the cataclysmic oil shocks of 1973 and 1979, and the rise of huge "syndicated" loans to the Third World.

Marron analyzes the effects of the May 1, 1975, deregulatory event, when fixed commission rates on stock market transactions were abolished. This, in turn, resulted in a shakeout of medium-sized securities firms and the acquisition of many others. He traces the effect of the deregulation on Japan, the

United Kingdom, and West Germany, and concludes that deregulation is the single most important factor in the development of the global capital market.

He also focuses on the increased strategic role of computers in world finance. Illustrating their impact, he traces the development of NASDAQ, which now has an overall trading value of 29 billion shares, with a total value of $378 billion, and predicts that NASDAQ will be the model for tomorrow's global stock exchange. He also predicts the development of truly 24-hour, seven-day-a-week markets, linking together exchanges on different continents and handling world-class stocks.

Under the heading of "An Explosion of Choices," Marron traces the effect of deregulation, industry consolidation, and increasing competition as the source of "financial supermarkets." By contrast, he defines the PaineWebber philosophy, which focuses on a few business lines with a high quality of service rather than on diversification.

The globalization economy is defined by the activities of three principal trading centers: New York, London, and Tokyo. Wall Street is three times the size of Tokyo's exchange, eight times the size of London's, and today boasts half of the world's corporate value. He stresses the importance of the United Kingdom as a financial center but predicts that the Japanese will play a central role in the world of global finance as the Japanese consumer electronics and automobile industries have done in their respective industry sectors.

Marron defines the consolidation of wealth within the control of institutional investors as a dominant factor, since they now account for 50 percent of daily trading on the New York Stock Exchange, and on some days for as much as 70 percent. In fact, institutions are estimated to hold 44 percent of the market value of all U.S. stocks.

In the latter part of the chapter, Marron outlines the services offered by his own firm, PaineWebber, and describes its place in the global marketplace. He outlines some of the risks of globalization and voices some concern about the fallibility of self-regulation. He believes, nevertheless, that the advantages of a deregulated, computerized, securitized global marketplace clearly offset the risks.

ORGANIZING FOR AND MEETING THE GLOBAL CHALLENGE (Dr. Karlheinz Kaske)

From a modest beginning in 1847, Siemens AG has become one of the world's largest electrical and electronic companies, operating in 127 countries. Dr. Karlheinz Kaske, president and chief executive officer, notes that the company established its first businesses abroad in St. Petersburg (now Leningrad) and in London in the 1860s. Then, in 1881, representatives of Siemens met with Thomas Edison and developed a relationship that led to the manufacture by Siemens of filament lamps for European markets and the opening of offices in Chicago and New York City.

From these early origins, Siemens has grown into a highly sophisticated and sensitive multinational, with strong convictions as to the meaning, value, and positive effect of international trade. Kaske sees the elimination of trade barriers in recent decades as responsible for the prosperity and high growth rates of participating countries. He urges the continued liberalization of trade regulations and aggressive action by companies and nations to improve their performance through an increase in productivity and quality rather than through protectionist legislation.

The author sees the global challenge as more complex than many have imagined and recognizes social and political considerations as well as the economic tactics. He separates the global marketplace into two categories: (1) products and services that are sold the world over, irrespective of national markets and preferences, e.g., microchips, personal computers, or electric motors; and (2) global competition among a small number of companies dealing with highly specialized, selective markets requiring technological leadership and large capital resources, e.g., central office telephone switches or electric power generation systems.

Kaske observes that global competition tends to reduce the importance of the home market. For example, Siemens' home market only accounts for 6 percent of its worldwide market for industrial goods. The company copes with the global challenge by differentiating between its major markets, i.e., Western Europe and the United States, and the rest of the world, which consists of secondary markets. This, in turn, leads to a differentiation of the corporate role.

Kaske recognizes the intensification of international competition and stresses the importance of Siemens' long-term strategy: a combination of increased export efforts with simultaneous integration of the exporting company into the economies of the consuming countries. He notes the importance—and inevitability—of direct investments in the consuming countries, especially in manufacturing, and the follow-through in sales, installation, and service. Fifty percent of Siemens' international business rests on direct investment, and the percentage will increase.

The author discusses the importance of the global challenge on new organizational agreements and emphasizes the shift away from the classic structure, comprising a headquarters in the home market and dependent subsidiaries abroad. He contrasts this vertical relationship to the new horizontal relationship that has developed—interdependence between the home country and the overseas subsidiaries, functioning in a spirit of cooperation. He also believes that decentralization increases interdependence within each country and focuses more directly on local market needs and expectations.

In conclusion, Kaske notes the prevailing need for people who understand interdependence and who are willing to accept working partners in global activity. He points to a corporate culture attuned to a transnational, market-driven environment as the most important element to separate the winners from the losers.

TOWARD A GLOBAL INFORMATION AGE (James E. Olson)

The advent of a global information age is described by James E. Olson, former chairman of AT&T, in exciting and far-reaching terms. The convergence of computers and telecommunications has created new networks to carry information in all forms over superfast, high-capacity digital pathways. Increasingly, information is seen as a strategic asset for business, industry, and government, and those who can manage it effectively are seen as having a competitive advantage.

The world marketplace for consumer goods is both stimulated and supported by mass communication media. Harmonization of tastes and the internationalization of style and quality demands are reinforced by global information technology.

One section of this chapter describes the rise in information technology, citing the landmark dates of 1837 (Samuel Morse's invention of the telegraph), 1927 (Charles Lindbergh's transatlantic flight), and 1947 (Bell Labs' invention of the transistor). Olson expands our understanding of the technological revolution in recent decades and predicts awe-inspiring developments in the future.

He illustrates the force and effect of microcomputers in terms of miniaturization, speed, costs, reliability, and diversification. The pace of the advance of microelectronics is doubling our capabilities every 18 months—exponential growth that staggers the imagination and almost reads like science fiction. Olson predicts that the current rate of progress will produce a hundred million component chips by the turn of the century and that by 2020 a mere $4,000 investment in random access memory will store an entire 500,000-volume library—at less than one cent per book!

Olson discusses the impact of light-wave systems, which carry voice, video, data, and any other forms of information through ultrapure glass fibers the diameter of a human hair. This will improve the cost and the performance of international communications and will certainly intensify the level of global competition.

The global information, management, and movement market is about $500 billion today and will exceed $880 billion by 1990, whereas the U.S. domestic market for telecommunications equipment and services, as well as computers and computer services, is projected to nearly double, from $224 billion in 1985 to $400 billion in the next five years. These investment data reflect the growing levels of demand for information and the growth prospects within these industries.

Consistent with many of the coauthors in this volume, Olson stresses the need for strategic alliances with major foreign firms. He describes joint ventures and partnerships with Olivetti of Italy, N.V. Philips of the Netherlands; British Telecom; Kokusai Denshin Denwa, Ltd. of Japan; Nordic Cable and Wire of Denmark; Goldstar Semiconductor of the Republic of Korea; and others. These are some of the more than 20 partnerships that AT&T has to market or manufacture products abroad.

In summary, AT&T is responding to the global market in three major ways: (1) strengthening its international communications services, (2) marketing equipment to government-owned and private companies, and (3) concentrating on businesses and governments that need information movement and management systems in Western Europe, the Far East, and North America.

QUALITY AND EFFICIENCY—THE KEYS TO THE GLOBAL MARKET (Paul H. O'Neill)

This chapter by Paul H. O'Neill, chairman of ALCOA, is an upbeat discussion of world competition and its lasting effect on the United States. O'Neill firmly believes that this country can reemerge as a driving force in world competition and that the most dramatic and overriding change required is a change in perspective, namely a shift from the domestic perspective of the past to a global perspective.

A variety of explanations has been offered for the poor showing of the United States in global economic competition, but these simply rationalize our position. Two basic requirements must underpin an effective global outlook, says the author: quality and efficiency. He recognizes that American products have improved in quality and that operations have continued to improve, but he believes, nevertheless, that the gap with foreign competition has not yet been closed. "Better than last year isn't good enough anymore," he says, nor is "better than our domestic competition." The challenge today, at a time when customer demand is driven by quality rather than price, is to be better than the rest of the world.

O'Neill draws on his experience as former president of the International Paper Company and his chairmanship of Alcoa in discussing the high expectations established by the Japanese. These cannot be met, he says, by rationalizing or by making excuses. O'Neill sees the Japanese standards as legitimate and serving to systematically increase performance in manufacturing processes, operational controls, and quality results. He does not believe that these standards raise costs and reduce productivity but rather that they improve output, lower manufacturing costs, and result in less scrap product.

The author expresses concern with the effect on U.S. competitiveness of taxes and regulatory policies. He emphasizes the necessity for government efficiency, but he does not turn to government for a solution to the problem of U.S. competitiveness. He clearly believes that the solution rests most properly on the shoulders of the private sector in the United States and that "shielding U.S. firms from the best foreign competition will only insure that we will become a second-rate nation in the next century."

The author identifies four clear "threads" that account for the pattern of success of foreign competitors.

- Doing a better job in the utilization of human resources.
- Having a fixation on quality. Whereas, U.S. companies provide long warranties, foreign competition makes products that last.
- Paying serious attention to the detail of every activity every day, including manufacturing, marketing, finance, labor relations, and so on. "There are no unimportant or less important activities in the work of successful foreign competitors."
- Having a shorter cycle time to translate better ideas into everyday practice.

In conclusion, O'Neill is not sanguine that individual companies can meet the challenge of global competition through financial restructuring, plant closings, or reorganization. Instead, he says, they must make fundamental changes in the traditional business systems in order to achieve and sustain improved quality and efficiency.

GROWING TO SERVE THE GLOBAL MARKETPLACE (Edmund T. Pratt, Jr.)

Pfizer Inc. was founded as a small family business in Brooklyn, New York, in 1849. Edmund T. Pratt, Jr., chairman and chief executive officer, traces the early history and development of this organization to its present status as a leading multinational pharmaceuticals corporation with $5 billion in sales and 40,000 employees. Pfizer operates in 140 countries and has a manufacturing presence in 65.

The international character of Pfizer's business philosophy is typified by the fact that the investments are primarily managed by nationals in each country. Only 75 employees are expatriates of a total work force of 40,000—and fewer than half of these are American.

Pratt describes the great changes in Pfizer that have occurred since 1941. It expanded from a chemical company operating almost exclusively in the United States to a multinational company, manufacturing and marketing a wide variety of products in every part of the world. He notes the increased complexity of government regulations and the need for house counsel and continuing litigation. For example, the entire development and approval process for Terramycin was completed in one year in the early 1950s, whereas today this process for a new drug runs seven to ten years and costs an average of $125 million.

Changes in international commercial relationships and their effects on consumption patterns have been even more profound. Partially, says Pratt, they are related to the contraction of time and space through jet travel. Travel by Americans to other parts of the world grew 13-fold, from 1950 to 1985, whereas foreign travel to the United States grew 33-fold, from 242,000 in 1950 to over 8 million by the mid-1980s. These changes were also reflected in the expansion of world trade, the growth of both exports and imports, and the massive movement of capital among nations. U.S. assets abroad increased to almost $900 billion, or over 400 percent, whereas foreign investment in U.S. assets increased 1,100 percent, to almost $800 billion. The global economy is now an established fact.

One fundamental change in consumer behavior, says Pratt, is

the worldwide demand for the same sorts of goods and services—especially among the industrial nations—posing a new set of problems for the multinational corporation.

Pratt groups these problems under "direct" and "indirect" effects. The more direct effects of governmental policies include: the new drug approval process in the United States; the policy of encouraging "generic" drug substitution and its adverse effect on research and development; the prevalence of third-party payment of medical bills, with potentially adverse effects on health-care quality; and other macroeconomic policies in fiscal, monetary, legal, and trade areas. Finally, he discusses the regulatory challenge of managing in 160 different countries, with differing regulations, price controls, and limits on direct investment.

The indirect effects of government policies include currency fluctuation and the failure to protect intellectual property rights. The latter problem is spelled out to illustrate the flagrant disregard and open piracy of patents, trademarks, and copyrights, which rob Pfizer and companies like Pfizer, of their foremost competitive advantage—their technology. Pratt espouses fair treatment for all parties in the genuine interest of international trade and a better world for all.

MEETING THE CHALLENGE OF THE 21ST CENTURY (Tadahiro Sekimoto)

Tadahiro Sekimoto, president of the NEC Corporation, characterizes NEC as a world enterprise determined to lead the way into the twenty-first century with C&C—that is, the integration of computers and communications.

To achieve this objective, NEC is committed to four management principles in four basic business areas: computers, communications, home electronics, and detection devices. The four management principles that underly the drive toward internationalization include: foresight, action, staying power, and flexibility.

Sekimoto traces the development and expansion of NEC toward a truly world enterprise, from 1950 to the present, and forecasts the course of NEC's future development. Expansion and growth have been based upon a combination of foreign acquisitions, corporate reorganization, new marketing bases, and new manufacturing facilities. The result: business dealings in 144 countries, 26 offices in 25 countries, 23 sales companies in 14 countries, 20 production companies and 24 plants in 13 countries, and a total of 17,500 overseas employees. Worldwide sales exceeded $13 billion in fiscal 1986, with total employment of 96,000.

This 40-year span was comprised of several distinct phases. The foundation for overseas activities was set in the 1950s; in the next decade, NEC gained a footing as an international firm; and in the current decade, it has expanded its operations as a world enterprise.

Sekimoto also remarks upon the need for technology transfers as an inducement to major international business breakthroughs. Localized production is considered important as are joint ventures and the ultimate creation of production and marketing networks overseas.

In the concluding section of this chapter, Sekimoto discusses the contemporary trade frictions that arise as a result of the intensity of international economic competition. In response to these forces, he notes that NEC's products—computers and communications—are the infrastructure on which an information society rests and that exporting such equipment can be a form of positive economic exchange. Another response to friction is NEC's concern for localization, evidenced by the fact that only 3 percent of NEC's 17,500 overseas employees have been sent from Japan; that, in terms of capital, Japan has been willing to accept minority equity participation; and that NEC prefers to use locally procured parts "after a careful consideration of quality." Finally, the author voices a genuine preference for international exchanges to increase understanding and cooperation and to promote world peace.

COMPETITION IN THE WORLD ECONOMY (Colby Chandler)

Colby Chandler, chairman and CEO of the Eastman Kodak Company, sees the international trade and financial crisis as a tri-level problem, involving (1) macroeconomic policies, (2) the debt burden of developing countries, and (3) the diminished lead of the United States in world competition.

Complacency or complaints are negative and lead to counterproductive responses, Chandler believes. Rather, he calls for public and private policies that will maximize the U.S. ability to compete without isolating or insulating the nation from the world marketplace. Chandler calls for a multilateral trading system with checks and balances, and negotiated agreements with our trading partners that include expanded coverage for services, investment, subsidies, and intellectual property.

He urges the government to avoid protectionist solutions, to sponsor research and development with both commercial and defense uses, to support a first-rate education system to generate a well-trained, educated work force, and to be sensitive to the effect of excessive regulation on competitiveness.

Chandler places the primary responsibility, however, on the corporation. He applauds restructuring to maintain fitness and defines four practices to achieve world-class status: (1) a significant, high-quality research effort; (2) a business unit structure that permits rapid transformation of the fruits of research into commercially viable quality products; (3) a worldwide strategy of investment, production, and marketing; and (4) the ability to monitor and improve both quality and cost. These goals have provided the underpinning for Kodak's success.

Chandler has reorganized the CEO's office, delegated responsibility, decentralized, refocused research and development, and encouraged an interest in change, competitiveness, and quality. The process of innovative product development, manufacturing, and marketing have been upgraded by a new organization structure that delegates decision making to business units run by managers with vertically integrated worldwide responsibility. Research and development has been realigned to link up with both technology and business strategies. The result has been the telescoping of new product development lead times from a previous five- to seven-year span to two-year spans. The new nine-volt lithium battery illustrates this decisive leadership in technology.

Kodak now seeks a broad range of products, with a long-range continuum of funding adequate to ensure future profitability. Kodak introduced 56 new photographic products in 1986, more than in any year in its long history. It consolidated older product lines, targeting 25 percent for elimination. The focus today is on manufacturing products of consistent quality worldwide and includes a major investment in training.

Chandler believes that American corporations have their work cut out in remaining competitive in today's economy. But he also believes that they can meet the challenge. Kodak, for one, is well on its way to doing so.

NEW DIRECTIONS IN SWEDISH MANAGEMENT (Anders Lindström)

In his chapter on The Carnegie Group of Stockholm, Sweden, Anders Lindström, managing director and chief executive officer, discusses the impact of new directions in management and multinational operations from both a broad national perspective and from the perspective of an individual firm.

Changes in Swedish management style are attributed to the following characteristics of the Swedish economy:

- The existence of a well-disciplined labor movement linked to the Social Democratic Party has resulted in increased participation of workers in industrial actions.
- Heavy dependence upon exports to maintain the Swedish welfare society has acted as a force for change in managerial techniques.
- Concern for education, human welfare, and individual rights has increased social activism.

Lindström identifies and describes the changes in management style in terms of four factors: employees motivation, decentralization, joint ventures with foreign partners, and information and communications within the firm.

- A deep concern for *employee motivation* underlies the conviction of Swedish management that high productivity is dependent upon employee participation. Two approaches are presented: (1) a flow of information regarding company objectives, strategies, and operations is maintained in the form of a "dialog" with employees; and (2) employees receive increased financial rewards, through bonus systems and participation in the company's growth through stock ownership.
- *Decentralization* has become the inevitable by-product of expansion, diversification and internationalization. Product-oriented business areas have been defined as profit centers. This in turn has led to downsizing of the headquarters staff and forced delegation of authority. At the same time, financial controls are retained at the top.
- *Joint ventures* with foreign partners are a relatively recent trend. The need for such corporate changes has been created by the high cost of technical development programs (R&D), increasingly severe competition in world markets for capital goods, and the erosion of confidence that companies can compete by "going it alone." This trend mirrors the multitude of new joint ventures that are blossoming throughout the industrial countries.
- *Sharing of information* with all employees has been transformed from a philosophy of secretiveness to a proactive management determination to educate and inform employees with regularity and thoroughness. Here the Work Councils play an important part. Employee attitude surveys have become the vogue. The need for international financing has forced more meaningful financial reporting and disclosure.

These four basic trends are illustrated by Lindström's discussion of the Bahco story—a case history of his direction of the reorganization and turnaround of a medium-sized Swedish engineering products company. In 1983, he assumed the role of CEO in a company awash in red ink and in only two years managed to institute a series of radical changes that saved the business and assured the company's future.

THE INTERNATIONALIZATION OF
FINANCIAL MARKETS (John F. McGillicuddy)

In this discussion of the profound economic developments that have internationalized the credit and capital markets, John F. McGillicuddy, chief executive officer of Manufacturers Hanover, points out that "theory has become stark reality." This economic revolution, he says, has created the ability to access money anywhere in the world to finance investments anywhere in the world. Money crosses continents and national boundaries at breathtaking speed, financing the global race for markets and profits.

This chapter and Donald Marron's chapter, written from the perspective of the CEO of a financial services company, reinforce each other. Although both writers discuss the global financial marketplace, McGillicuddy observes it as chief executive of a bank with full operating presence in 32 of the world's major financial centers, from Bahrain to Buenos Aires, from Manila to Madrid. In fact, he stresses the need to function as an indigenous bank in each country and, despite the emergence of global electronic banks, to localize, paralleling the actions of multinational manufacturers.

Globalization of financial markets has created the economic interdependence of nations without similar political interdependence. He draws our attention to the critical role played by foreign purchases of U.S. Treasury securities in financing our national debt. By 1986, foreign purchases of Treasury securities accounted for nearly one quarter of such sales, up from only 4 percent in 1983.

The author also cites the ripple effect of global financial markets on American manufacturers, noting that exchange rates by 1983 had overvalued the dollar and taxed our exports by 25 percent, subsidized imports by a like amount, and resulted in the largest trade gap in our history. Recent reversals of this condition have been dependent upon a weaker dollar.

McGillicuddy guides the reader through the recent internationalization of credit and capital markets by defining the frenzy of financial innovation. He clarifies the "zoological acronyms" of CATS, TIGERS, STAGS, and ZEBRAS—new forms of financial investments that have appeared on the international landscape. In 1985 alone, some 20 new credit and capital market investments were introduced in four main groupings—funding, underwriting, hedging, and arbitraging instruments. Conversant with the creative innovations of the world of high finance, the author describes the staggering growth of international bond issues—up to $225 billion in 1986 (as opposed to $47 billion in 1983), denominated in no less than 16 different currencies.

McGillicuddy analyzes the forces behind the internationalization of credit and capital markets as a confluence of three interconnected forces: (1) information technology, (2) new financial techniques to respond to unprecedented volatility in the behavior of interest rates and currency rates, and (3) financial deregulation, including the breaking down of national barriers to money and capital flows.

Information technology. Major banks and other financial institutions have put into place their own global communications networks. This information technology evolved from a supportive system of domestic customer servicing to an international strategic program. Massive investments by U.S. commercial banks on systems technology reached $8.2 billion in 1985. Global electronic banks have been developed with three things in common: (1) a broad, worldwide network of branches or subsidiaries that function as indigenous banks; (2) a global communications network linking overseas offices and creating a pool of global information; and (3) hardware and software capabilities to allow customers to access the bank's internal information systems on a real-time basis.

He describes this communications network as the advent of banking's "global village," resulting in the movement of a large pool of money around the world at the speed of sound. McGillicuddy calls this a "high-tech money pump," which circulates in excess of $1 trillion each day.

New financial techniques. Electronic technology increased the velocity and volume of money floats and also changed the nature of the credit process and the role of financial intermediation. Two important techniques resulted: *disintermediation* and *securitization.* In today's context, these terms refer not only to the outflow of bank deposits and other investment instruments, but to the outflow of more and more money directly from suppliers of funds to users of funds. Credit itself is being disintermediated. "Securitization" is the new term in the financial lexicon—turning nonmarketable debt into marketable debt. Through securitization, assets formerly held on a lender's books are packaged and converted into blocks of securities that the originating institution sells to other investors, most commonly, insurance companies, pension funds, and other banks. This method has become applicable to megabuck loans in connection with leveraged buyouts and to other transactions that "securitize everything that moves," as one journalist has observed.

Deregulation. This trend is seen as the handmaiden of globalization and innovation and is directly related to market volatility and real rates of interest (e.g., the spread of nominal interest rates and the rate of inflation). One dramatic illustration of the effects of deregulation was the almost total lifting five years ago of consumer interest-rate ceilings on bank deposits. According to Mr. McGillicuddy, who was in the eye of the storm, deregulation turned retail banking on its head and opened a floodgate of new competition and new products. Naturally, he reflects on this radical change as a dangerous disintermediation of the banking system. True deregulation, he believes, would remove existing artificial barriers—namely, the Glass-Steagall Act—and allow commercial banks to underwrite most securities, while extending commercial banking powers to investment banks.

Roger B. Smith

Roger B. Smith became chairman and chief executive officer of General Motors in January 1981. He is also chairman of GM's Finance Committee and a member of the Executive and Administration Committees. Prior to being elected chairman, Mr. Smith had been an executive vice president and member of the GM board of directors since December 1974.

Mr. Smith received his bachelor's degree and master's degree from the University of Michigan in 1947 and 1949, respectively. He began his GM career in 1949. After a series of promotions, he became treasurer of the corporation in 1970 and vice president in charge of financial staff and a member of the administrative committee in 1971. In 1974, he was elected executive vice president, with responsibility for the financial, public relations, and industry-government relations staffs. In February 1978, Mr. Smith originated the General Motors Cancer Research Awards. He serves as chairman of the General Motors Cancer Research Foundation, which administers the awards.

Mr. Smith is a trustee of the California Institute of Technology, Cranbrook Educational Community, and the Michigan Colleges Foundation, Inc. He has received honorary doctorates from several universities. A member of the boards of directors of Johnson & Johnson and Citicorp, Mr. Smith is also chairman of the Business Roundtable. He is a member of the Business Council, the Society of Automotive Engineers, the Advertising Council's Industries Advisory Committee, as well as other civic and professional organizations.

1
GLOBAL COMPETITION—
A STRATEGY FOR SUCCESS

Roger B. Smith
Chairman and Chief Executive Officer
General Motors Corporation, USA

America is now in the midst of one of its greatest challenges in history—a competitive struggle that will determine whether our standard of living remains the envy of the world and whether we retain our current role as the world's preeminent economic power. This challenge is less visible than the wars that in our past threatened our very existence as a nation and our fundamental freedoms. But its outcome is no less vital to our future.

The central question facing us is whether America can compete successfully in the world marketplace. With all we have going for us, can we restore our industrial competitiveness? Or will we let it slip away—and along with it our national wealth and power?

Despite all the dire conclusions we hear about our country's loss of competitiveness and waning economic power, I am convinced America's best days still lie ahead. But we will reach them only if we acknowledge that global changes have occurred and act decisively to make the changes in our own country that meet these new demands.

American industry has a major role to play in all this. But it cannot do the job alone. Government must create the climate within which industry can act to restore its competitiveness. And labor must contribute its share.

The starting point for all our efforts must be a recognition that economic power no longer rests in the hands of one nation or one region of the world. Economic interdependence is now a fact of life. One indicator of that interdependence is the rapid growth of world trade. Over the past 25 years, world trade has been growing about 70 percent faster than the growth rate of the world GNP. This growth of trade has brought to the citizens of those countries who have allowed themselves to be open to it an abundance and variety of goods unparalleled in history.

However, rapidly expanding trade has posed difficult challenges as well. It has forced firms whose market positions once seemed invulnerable into competitive struggles that threaten their viability. The management of these firms and the workers they employ have reexamined long-held assumptions about what makes for competitive success. Painful adjustments have occurred.

The auto industry has been one where change has been massive and where adjustments are still working themselves out. In this chapter, I want to describe what General Motors is doing to respond to the immense challenge it faces. I believe we have developed a strategy that will allow us to compete successfully with anyone in the world. We are putting this strategy into place now, and the results will soon be evident.

I also want to discuss what must be done by our government to enable America to restore its competitiveness as a nation. It is important to distinguish between competitiveness of American firms and the competitiveness of America. Since the mid-1960s, America's competitiveness has clearly declined. Our share of manufactured exports has fallen by any measure you want to use. But during the same period, the share of manufactured exports accounted for by American multinational firms has remained virtually constant. This suggests that what has been occurring over the last 20 years is not the decline of American management or American technology, but the erosion of the relative attractiveness of America as a place to engage in manufacturing. Restoring a favorable business climate to this country should be a major priority of government.

THE AUTO INDUSTRY IN GLOBAL COMPETITION

The U.S. auto industry packs an enormous economic punch. It directly affects the livelihood of about one in every six American workers. The auto industry has become internationalized to an extent undreamed of just 20 years ago. Decisions made in Tokyo, or Wolfsburg, or Detroit have repercussions around the world.

In the auto industry, competition is concentrated in what are called the TRIAD nations. These three centers of auto production are in North America, Japan, and Europe. These regions account for more than 600 million people—only 15 percent of the world's population—but the gross national products of these regions make up 72 percent of the free world economy.

Of particular importance to our industry is the fact that these nations produce 90 percent of the world's motor vehicles. And now, more of that productive capacity is moving to the United States. By 1990, so-called Japanese "transplants," Japanese automakers who are now manufacturing cars in the U.S., will be making more than one and a half million vehicles in the U.S. If current projections are correct, the number of assembly plants in North America will increase from 52 to 61 in the next three years. Of course, this will only add to the intense competitive atmosphere in this country and will almost certainly create overcapacity in the industry—too many cars being built and not enough market demand. Some analysts believe this overcapacity could reach over two million cars annually.

There is very little in the way of economic advantage that separates the competition in this struggle. For example, the cost of most raw materials used in the auto industry is nearly the same for both foreign and domestic manufacturers. Even though it costs the Japanese roughly $1,000 less to produce compact and midsize cars, the labor rates in Japan, Europe, and the United States are moving much closer together.

One element that will set the competition apart—one element that will determine the winners and losers in the global marketplace—is technology. But even technology alone won't make the total difference. It must be incorporated with human innovation to be effective. I believe the company that can best unleash the innovative power of its people, while at the same time channeling these innovations for the good of the company, will gain the advantage in the global marketplace. Effectively combining people and technology is the greatest management challenge facing American industry as we head into the next century.

GM'S GLOBAL STRATEGY

At GM, hardly any part of our worldwide corporation—roughly 800,000 employees working in 38 countries—has remained untouched in our drive to meet that challenge by putting the best available technology together with the most technically literate workers in the business.

To prepare for this global battle, we've created a strategic plan to improve our competitive position in four major ways: by strengthening our human resources, expanding our technological expertise through new business acquisitions and mergers in related key industries, achieving world-class cost and quality in manufacturing, and developing new marketing strategies. You might call it our blueprint for future success.

The Human Factor

The first part of GM's blueprint begins with our people. We have some very ambitious goals that demand the best of our management team, our employees, and the whole GM organization. We are trying to change our whole corporate culture—to move a giant worldwide organization toward a more flexible, decentralized management in order to gain better decisions and greater participation by employees at every level. But developing the plan is really the easy part for any corporation. The hard part is implementing it in a management environment that has been so successful for so long that the traditionalists in the organization find it difficult to see why we should change at all. Managers must believe in the plan, buy into it, and make it work. And you have to give it time to work.

This is especially true with technology. Through patience and perseverance, we've learned that technology must be introduced with the full recognition that technology is only as good as the people who run it and live with it day in and day out. Solid human partnerships between management and employees and the most advanced thinking in workplace organization are necessary for the implementation of technology. They are the bedrock on which successful high technology systems will be built.

We're building these human partnerships, in part, through the team concept approach, which brings employees and managers closer together when working towards a common goal. And that leads us to one of our greatest challenges. We are seeking ways to combine people and machines to achieve efficiencies that deliver the best product to our customers at a price they can afford and which will provide a satisfactory profit for the business and its stockholders.

GM's Saturn Corporation will play an important role in changing the management structure and decision making within the factory in the next decade. Under the Saturn system, union and worker participation will reach a new plateau in the auto industry.

Skeptics point out that there are several risks in this innovative management concept. For example, they say friction could result when committees determine pay and bonuses for all employees. Others claim that management gives up too much of its authority and decision-making responsibility. But overall, I think the potential benefits are worth the risks. And an important part of the Saturn concept is that it is flexible, and that's really the key element. If both the workers and management agree changes need to be made somewhere along the line, the system can always—and probably will be modified.

Besides affecting management style and structure, the growth in technology is also profoundly affecting our training needs. With our factories virtually exploding with new processes and new equipment, training the work force has become a lifelong process; there will be no graduation day from learning.

Our GM-UAW Human Resources Center, on the Auburn Hills campus of Michigan's Oakland Community College, is the hub for coordinating all design, development and implementation of our human resource programs. Trainer-representatives from different plants are brought in for instruction and carry what they learn to fellow workers back home. The center offers leadership training and preretirement programs along with health and safety training to help workers learn to handle hazardous materials and operate equipment safely. These programs will ultimately affect nearly 400,000 UAW-represented GM employees in nearly 150 plants.

Beyond practical training, we know that our employees must understand the challenges we're facing every day. To keep GM workers informed about the realities of global competition facing the auto industry—and all of American industry—groups of UAW local union leaders are taking part in seminars as part of a paid educational leave program. The groups hear presentations from economists, strategic planners, and congressmen about global economics and the emerging technological trends that are changing American industry. Many participants told us they had no idea American industry was facing such a serious threat from our foreign competitors.

On the salaried side, nearly 20,000 employees went through special training programs in 1985 to keep abreast of the latest technologies. These included classes on communications, technical, and management skill development.

These programs show how seriously GM is taking the job of training tomorrow's work force. But despite the efforts of management and labor, it's still no small task to get Americans to work together. We live in an adversarial society and in the past this was demonstrated dramatically in labor-management relations. But in a world society, we are competing with countries like Japan that, by culture and history, are oriented to consensus and uniformity. These are great strengths in Japanese industry. And in America, it is obvious that we can no longer afford the luxury of an excessively adversarial society. There's too much wasted effort, too much alienation between employees and management, and not enough effort to cooperate so our company can survive in dog-eat-dog worldwide competition. We need to combine the Japanese cooperative spirit with the American ability to think for oneself—we need to get the best of both worlds.

Acquisitions and Mergers

The second part of GM's four-part blueprint for the future is the goal of being the technological leader in our industry by expanding our business opportunities. In our plans to hold our competitive edge worldwide, we realized we couldn't continue to do things the way we had done them for the last 78 years. We knew we had to reach out beyond our own resources for the best technology and best thinking available—forming joint ventures and buying into other companies where necessary to make this happen. Two of the key building blocks were Electronic Data Systems and Hughes Aircraft, which we acquired in 1984 and 1985, respectively.

Electronic Data Systems, or EDS, is the largest and most technically advanced computer services company in the world. EDS is extremely knowledgeable in the development of software that can be used to control automated manufacturing systems. Since it is also the world leader in industrial communication networks, EDS is putting this knowledge to work to create the largest telecommunication network in the world. The network will eventually allow us to send voice, video, and data transmissions to all our GM offices and factories worldwide, as well as our dealers and suppliers. EDS and its computer experts are now helping to disseminate this new technology throughout GM.

A year after our EDS acquisition, we bought Hughes Aircraft to accelerate the application of electronics in our cars and give us direct access to the most advanced technology in American industry. Hughes is still an independent and autonomous company, but it is now part of a new business unit for GM's high-technology defense and electronics activities. The new unit also includes EDS, the Delco Electronics Corporation, and GM's defense operations and will promote even greater synergy among the operations in implementing advanced technology systems for GM products and plants worldwide.

Hughes technology will help us build new cars and trucks to outperform our competitors in terms of driveability, fuel economy, and safety. At the same time, these vehicles will provide superior information, communication, and entertainment systems. Hughes engineering skills are also assisting us in taking a total systems approach to our production and assembly operations. Such an approach will allow us to speed decision making, cut costs, improve product quality, and react more quickly to a changing marketplace.

GM has acquired or bought interests in a number of other

firms to help us achieve the goal of expanding our business opportunities. We have also entered into nearly 40 joint ventures since 1971 to improve our competitive position in the global marketplace. One of our most important steps in this direction was made with the Japanese automaker, Toyota.

We entered this agreement in 1983 to build the Chevrolet Nova, a new model based on a Toyota design, at our Fremont, California, facility. A new, independent company was formed, New United Motor Manufacturing, Incorporated (NUMMI). Splitting a $300 million investment down the middle gave us an opportunity to learn new manufacturing and management techniques from our Japanese partners with a relatively small expenditure of capital.

The importance of improved human relationships is one of the key lessons we've learned from the NUMMI joint venture. NUMMI uses significantly less automation than do many of GM's newer factories, and that shifts the emphasis to the need for good working relationships within the plant. The team concept is at the heat of the NUMMI system. By using the Japanese philosophy of kaizen, the constant search for improvement, team members are encouraged to find waste in machinery, materials, or methods of production, and then eliminate that waste.

Even the labor agreement at NUMMI is innovative. The contract provides for a cooperative problem-solving process, flexible work rules, and a commitment by both labor and management to work together to build the highest quality automobile in the world at the lowest possible cost to the consumer.

NUMMI is just one example of how a company can use joint ventures to improve its own operations and reduce its costs in a highly competitive marketplace. Among our other joint ventures, one of the most promising agreements is with South Korean automaker Daewoo. In this 50-50 arrangement, Daewoo is manufacturing the new LeMans for Pontiac, which will handle distribution and marketing in the U.S. This project is truly international in scope, with GM's Adam Opel unit in Germany designing the car, the South Koreans building it, and Americans and Koreans selling it.

Throughout the auto industry and the American business

community, joint ventures are increasingly important to survival in the global marketplace. In my own industry, the bottom line of the joint venture phenomenon is simply this: no vehicle manufacturer today can be an island. Increasingly, companies like General Motors will be cooperating with other companies around the world to build better products to serve their customers and at reduced costs. The industry will be stronger as a result. And while employment in the U.S. auto industry will decrease over the next few years, joint ventures will help insure the security of the large majority of our remaining employees and those with supplier companies.

Building the Best

The third key part of our blueprint to beat the competition is winning the cost-and-quality battle. And again, people and technology are the key elements. The quality outlook at GM can be summed up by what we call the "Four Absolutes of Quality Management."

First, quality is not how well you do something, it's whether you do the job needed to meet your requirements. Second, you don't improve quality by increased emphasis on quality inspections. You must change the system so that products are built right the first time. You shouldn't wait for a problem to occur and then try to fix it. Third, the performance standard must be zero defects; anything less would be admitting you can't do world-class work. And fourth, the measure of quality is the price of non-conformance. For example, you have to measure how much it is costing you not to meet the zero-defects standard. In the auto industry, that cost can be more than 10 percent of sales and includes warranty, quality control, engineering, scrap, and, most importantly, lost sales due to poor quality.

On the cost side, we've introduced leading-edge technology into our plants to improve our productivity. By reducing the hours it takes to manufacture a car, our costs will drop significantly. For example, a $2.5 billion stamping press modernization program is now showing results at our Mansfield, Ohio, stamping plant. We're using some of the latest technology from West Germany and Japan to improve our die-change time on some of the world's largest transfer presses. Die changes, which used to take up to a day to complete, are now done in a matter of minutes. These presses now turn out virtually perfect-quality parts at a rate of 100 million a year.

We've also made major steps forward with new competitive labor agreements we've negotiated with the United Auto Workers Union—and many others we're working on now. These agreements not only have reduced costs, but have reduced the number of job classifications, and improved quality. These agreements also help us keep jobs in the U.S. rather than exporting them to countries where the costs of production are typically lower.

Most of the gains being made in improved cost and quality are coming from new ways of engineering, manufacturing, and assembling vehicles, new working relationships in the plants, new plant designs, and totally integrated facilities. One project that rolls these all into one is GM's new Saturn Corporation, designed to produce a completely new American car in a new way. It's a project aimed at proving that America can be competitive in cost and quality on a worldwide basis.

Saturn's highly integrated manufacturing and assembly complex is being built in Spring Hill, Tennessee, after a much-publicized site selection process.

The Saturn approach can be described in two words— simultaneous engineering. It was inspired by two realities. First, it was taking too long to get new products from the drawing board to the showroom. Second, we had far too many costly product changes too late in the design process, and this was expensive, contributed to poor quality, and delayed the market introduction of our new cars.

With simultaneous engineering, the car and all component designs go along parallel tracks. Everyone is involved at the outset—designers, manufacturing engineers, suppliers, and quality and service specialists. It's really an experiment in people management with every employee a decision maker— that means, for example, every manager, every machine operator, and every skilled tradesman.

When the Saturn Corporation begins production, its message to the rest of General Motors, to other U.S. businesses, and to the world will be: "We can do it right, we can compete with the best in the world."

Another project that will keep us at the leading edge of technological growth and moving along the path to be the best in the world is the heavily-automated Factory of the Future. In this factory, manufacturing functions are tied to computers that guide the process bringing raw materials in one door and finished products out another.

Production is done by robots under the watchful eye of human supervisors. The factory is so flexible that the machinery can be changed from assembling one model to another within a matter of minutes. That compares to changeovers that normally take days or even weeks to complete.

The first factory of this type has begun operation at a GM facility in Saginaw, Michigan. It costs about 30 percent more than a conventional plant of the same size. But the added cost will be recovered in lower labor costs, reduced waste, more effective inventory controls, and improved quality.

Saturn and the Factory of the Future will provide many of the ideas that will lead GM into the next century. The manufacturers who successfully integrate the ideas they learn from forward-thinking projects like these will achieve a significant competitive advantage. In contrast, I believe the auto manufacturers who can't compete on a worldwide basis in the next decade—or the next century—will be those who decide either not to get in the technology race and explore new ideas—or decide not to stay there.

Right now, U.S. manufacturers are making an enormous effort to modernize their 50-year-old industrial base with state-of-the-art technology. At GM we've completely renovated 19 old plants and build eight new assembly plants since 1979. This has allowed us to announce plans to close 11 other plant operations as part of a coordinated modernization program developed in the late 1970's.

On a worldwide scale, GM's capital expenditures from 1981 through 1987 have totaled more than $55 billion—spending that's critical to our technology plans.

In the long-run, we know moves like these will help us lead the development of new technology that will allow us to stay ahead of the change curve and the competition.

Marketing

Our blueprint for success so far has included greater development of our human resources, new business opportunities to improve our technological capabilities, and world-class cost and quality. But without innovative people developing new marketing strategies for our products as well, we still won't be a world competitive organization.

Effective marketing is an ever-increasing premium in today's auto industry. The total vehicle market is truly global, with diverse tastes reflecting different demographic, geographic, and psychographic forces. Vehicle offerings from worldwide competitors are expanding both ends of the price spectrum, and are becoming more feature competitive with new generations of options. Truck products have much broader appeal, but also are more complex because of the large number of special options required. With new features and greater versatility, trucks are blurring the traditional distinctions between cars and commercial vehicles, particularly in the small truck business.

In North America, global competitors are aggressively seeking to share in the world's biggest and most lucrative automotive market. Old brand and product loyalties are falling by the wayside as customers become more sophisticated and now have more than 600 different models to choose from.

GM's marketing strategy in the face of this competition is to be the most market-driven, consumer-oriented company in the industry and to provide the most exciting and rewarding ownership experience. We have a rich heritage of being the industry's leading marketer, going back to the 1920's and Alfred P. Sloan's plan of a car for "every purse and purpose."

One way GM has responded to the marketplace was the reorganization in 1984 of our North American vehicle operations. Recognizing structural changes that had occurred in the market, we reshaped our six car divisions into marketing and product planning entities. This reorganization more sharply focused the goals of the divisions and redirected their attention to the fundamental questions of "who are we, who are our customers, what is our mission, and what are the basic products to best express our identity?"

The reorganization also allowed us to integrate advanced engineering and manufacturing into a single unit, thus eliminating overlaps and creating a more effective team for those who design and manufacture cars.

This reorganization was not just aimed at improving internal efficiencies, but also to make GM more customer-driven. Distinct divisional brand and core product images are targeted at specific consumer groups in order to best meet their needs in terms of enhanced product image differentiation.

Our ability to respond rapidly to the market depends on our overall capability in market research and advertising. An example of GM's strategic use of market research is our redefined segmentation of car and light-commercial vehicle classifications. This new segmentation of the market is the underlying support for the marketing and product planning goals of our North American vehicle groups. It "maps" the targeted divisional roles, missions, and images against the various criteria in the consumer's purchase decisions.

In North America, GM will reduce the number of models and increase market penetration by emphasizing the divisions' core products and minimizing the overlap of other models. At the same time, this strategy will increase the number of vehicles unique to each division, strengthening the divisional images by marketing cars that are in harmony with each division's theme. Similar efforts are also under way overseas.

With our market truly global—and the customer's taste far more discriminating—advertising appeals based on brand or national loyalty are no longer necessarily effective. Fewer people today want to buy American, or French, or German, as much as they want to satisfy their life-style needs. Need fulfillment becomes the primary factor in the purchase decision, and our vehicle divisions are accelerating their efforts in segmented or targeted advertising to meet these demands.

Given the large amounts spent for advertising by American businesses each year, we need ever-improving productivity of spending in terms of value and results. Working with our advertising agencies and others, we must determine how better marketing and advertising can help us become more competitive by effectively demonstrating meaningful value to consumers. We must also find out how marketing and advertising can become more productive by delivering greater returns for each marketing dollar.

The marketing challenge of the next decade will be to identify and acquire relevant, accurate, easy-to-use, and cost-effective information needed to support key business decisions. Just as marketing provided a customer-based redrawing of the North American market segmentation, we look to marketing to identify future consumer "wants and needs" in product differentiation on an ongoing basis. This will enhance optimum use of our human and capital resources in meeting the needs of the marketplace.

The bottom line is the customer. The more sophisticated and diverse customers of the future will be demanding. So our ultimate goal for the 21st-century dealership is to provide a dealership environment, supported by advanced technology, that provides a simplified and pleasant sales experience for that customer.

GOVERNMENT'S ROLE

As I mentioned at the outset of this chapter, business cannot by itself restore America's competitiveness in international markets. The proper climate must exist to enable strategies of the sort I have just discussed to be carried out. It's been the absence of such a pro-competitive business climate that is responsible for much of the erosion of this country's manufacturing competitiveness.

When I talk about creating a climate to improve American competitiveness, I am not advocating what some have called "industrial policy." Rather than pick winners, I believe that government's job is to make sure that the underlying macroeconomic conditions, the conditions of the economy as a whole, are favorable to growth and productivity-enhancing investment, and to make sure the microeconomic interventions, actions taken in individual economic sectors, are sensible. Unfortunately, this country's recent experience demonstrates a lack of regard for both these requirements.

Macroeconomic Policies

In recent years, the climate in America for economic growth and investment has not been as favorable as in the economies of several of our major trading partners. The result has been a steady erosion of America's overwhelming advantage in productivity. When it first became evident that Japan's rate of growth was outstripping our own, this was attributed to their lower initial starting point. However, in about 1980, the average productivity level in Japanese manufacturing passed ours. Other countries are not far behind.

This would have been serious enough, but since 1980, our economy has struggled against an even greater government-created burden—a series of massive and persistent federal deficits that have doubled the national debt. These deficits have directly led to the current gross imbalance of trade and have undercut the competitiveness of many of America's most productive manufacturers. The continuing deficits are also setting the stage for a progressive weakening of our economy as we struggle to cope with a growing federal debt that must be dealt with.

The existence of this massive and still growing debt creates its own threat to restoring our competitiveness. The way we attracted the amount of foreign savings required to fund the record federal deficits of the last few years was by keeping our interest rates high. This, in turn, led to the strong dollar that devastated our exports and boosted our imports. Manufacturing had growing competitiveness problems before the dollar soared in the early 1980s. But this made them worse.

Fortunately, the dollar has declined sharply relative to the currencies of most of our major trading partners. This has begun to produce a reversal in our trade account. A major factor allowing the dollar to fall is the belief, spurred by the passage of the Gramm-Rudman Act, that the President and the Congress have become serious about controlling federal expenditures. The subsequent Supreme Court decision to rescind a critical portion of the Act undermined this belief to a degree. But progress shown in reducing the possible path of future federal budget deficits has restored confidence in the government's ability to get its fiscal house in order.

There is a real danger, however, that this encouraging progress will not be followed up. If the federal deficit were to stall at a level of $150 billion, the signal to foreign investors would be clear. U.S. interest rates would again rise in order to get these investors to hold U.S. government and private debt. This would reverse the decline in the dollar and the improvement in America's trade position this reversal generated. The result would be catastrophic to efforts to improve our competitiveness. It is for this reason I put deficit control at the very top of my agenda of macroeconomic imperatives.

The second imperative is to increase our nation's savings rate. The savings rate in Japan is so high that its government can run deficits that, as a share of GNP, exceed ours; domestic investment can remain strong; and the country can export sufficient capital to finance a considerable share of America's federal deficit. The last thing I would suggest is that we closely emulate Japan. In fact, one of their great needs is to change their own economic policy to stimulate domestic spending as a substitute for declining export growth. But we need to go part way.

The major change in our income tax system that was passed by Congress and signed by the President in 1986 will assist to some degree. The elimination of deductability of many forms of consumer interest ought to encourage saving. More importantly, the ending of many investment subsidies should increase the quality of investment.

Eventually, consideration may have to be given to making further changes in the structure of our tax system in order to reduce its pro-consumption bias. But for now, the most important thing is to avoid eroding the gains just won through the tax code revision. We must not allow tax rates to creep back up to where they become major influences over business and personal decision making. This means that the reduction of the federal deficit must be achieved primarily by a reduction in federal expenditures, not by increasing federal revenues. Moreover, we must not reintroduce the tax subsidies that have been so recently eliminated.

Microeconomic Policies

A critical feature of the business climate in any country is the microeconomic policies, the collection of government policies that influence individual decisions. Even if the share of GNP taken by the government in taxes is small, government actions can distort business decisions in significant ways.

The techniques that a country uses to raise tax revenues are one such set of policies that can either be productivity-enhancing or productivity-destroying. In my opinion, prior to the passage of the Tax Reform Act, the U.S. Internal Revenue Code was a productivity-destroying instrument. Though many of its features had been introduced for what must have seemed laudable reasons at the time, when combined with the high tax rates necessary to raise the increasing revenues the federal government had come to depend on, it became a regulatory monster, distorting the decision making of businessmen and consumers alike. In making investments, the question "what are its tax consequences?" was heard more often than "how will this improve our productivity?"

The restructuring of the tax code I just mentioned qualifies not only as a major shift in economic policy on the aggregate level, but also represents a major shift in the government's microeconomic policies. It was because of its favorable impact on removing tax consideration from business and personal decision making as well as its favorable overall economic impacts that General Motors strongly supported passage of this legislation.

A second area of microeconomic policy where much remains to be done is regulation. To be sure, some progress has been made in recent years in lessening the burden of government regulation. But few regulatory programs have been eliminated, even though the problems they were designed to deal with no longer exist.

Take, for example, the auto fuel economy regulations. Enacted when gasoline prices were being held at artificially low levels by government policies, these regulations were designed to spur the auto industry to design more fuel-efficient cars. Whether they or the eventual increase in gasoline prices were the most important factor in stimulating interest in energy conservation is a topic that can be debated endlessly. The point is that in today's climate, where gasoline prices show much greater signs of being market-determined, the original rationale for these regulations has disappeared.

The auto fuel economy regulations are only one example of

federal regulatory programs that have long outlived their usefulness. Yet efforts to eliminate or even simplify such programs meet with resistance. How can we expect American industry to become competitive internationally in such a difficult climate?

General Motors is not asking for an end to federal regulations affecting the automobile. But GM is asking that federal auto-related regulatory programs be conducted sensibly, with due consideration for their costs and for the burden they impose on the industry—a burden that goes far beyond dollars-and-cents calculations.

THE INGENUITY OF BUSINESS

Even if government does its share, America's ability to compete on a global scale ultimately depends on the ingenuity and determination of American business.

As Robert MacNeil of public television's "MacNeil-Lehrer Report" said: "America's future success in the world is going to be in large part determined by business. The military might of the United States cannot win a higher standard of living. Diplomats and politicians cannot negotiate it. Business is the bread and butter of democracy. It is what feeds and clothes and houses us. For most of the people it is the pursuit of happiness."

The important thing for us to remember is to keep our thoughts centered not on the bumps in the road, but on the broad avenue of economic opportunity that lies before us. With the proper technological moves and the right management choices, American business can have a great future—even in the face of the toughest global competition we've ever known. And I believe it's that combination of technology and people that is the key.

Business can lead our country into a whole new era, a renaissance of productivity and industrial innovation beyond even the wildest science fiction. Our job is to provide the leadership—as in the past—and we will.

Donald B. Marron

Donald B. Marron is chairman and chief executive officer of PaineWebber Group Inc. and chairman and chief executive officer of its major subsidiary, PaineWebber Incorporated.

Mr. Marron started his business career in 1951 with the New York Trust Company. In 1959 he formed D.B. Marron & Co., Inc., an investment banking firm. In 1965 the firm merged with Mitchell Hutchins & Co., Inc. Mr. Marron was named executive vice president of the merged firm in 1966 and in 1969 became its president. In May 1977 Mitchell Hutchins merged with PaineWebber, and Mr. Marron became president of PaineWebber Incorporated, the parent company. In June 1980 he was appointed chief executive officer and a year later was elected chairman.

In 1974 Mr. Marron was named by *Time* magazine as one of the outstanding leaders in America under the age of 45. In 1977 *Institutional Investor* magazine cited him among 100 individuals who most influenced the securities industry in the preceding decade. Mr. Marron is a recipient of the Special Service Award from the Citizens Union of the City of New York, the Skowhegan Gertrude Vanderbilt Whitney Award for significant contribution to the arts, and honorary doctorates from Baruch College and Long Island University.

Currently president of the board of trustees of the Museum of Modern Art and a trustee of both the Dana Foundation and the Trust for Cultural Resources of the City of New York, Mr. Marron is also a member of the Business Committee for the Arts, Inc., the Chief Executives Council, the Council on Foreign Relations, and the Governor's School and Business Alliance Task Force of New York.

2
THE GLOBALIZATION OF CAPITAL

Donald B. Marron
Chairman, President, and
Chief Executive Officer
PaineWebber Group, Inc., USA

ONE WORLD AND FOUR TRENDS

Over the past two decades, bankers, brokers, and indeed all of us in the financial community have learned firsthand what statesmen have been saying for a long time and what John Donne said best three centuries ago: no man is an island. Today, more than ever before, what happens in one nation, one sector of the economy, even one market touches everyone, everywhere. That this is so has enormous implications for the financial services industry, for each individual, and for our whole society. It presents us with many challenges as well as some risks—as the events of October 1987 vividly demonstrate—but also with many opportunities.

Even a casual reader of the *Wall Street Journal*, the *New York Times*, or the business and financial pages in any of a hundred other newspapers and magazines must be aware that the world of finance is in the midst of a period of extraordinary change.

Competition among the providers of financial services has never been more intense. The competitors are not limited to Wall Street and are increasingly not American. The number

53

and variety of the financial instruments they offer is simply staggering. How did all this come about? What are the changes that have taken place? What are their implications for the global capital market, for the various segments of the financial services industry, and for investors? These are some of the questions I'll be addressing in this chapter.

The recent history of the global capital marketplace has been dominated by several interrelated and mutually reinforcing trends. One of these is *globalization* itself: the increasing tendency of capital—of money in its various forms—to cross, recross, and almost to ignore national boundaries in the unceasing quest for maximum return. A second is *deregulation*: the dismantling of many of the rules and restrictions that long kept the financial world orderly and predictable, and the removal of which has created many investment opportunities and not a little marketplace turmoil. (Closely related to deregulation is a phenomenon known as disintermediation: the removal of banks as intermediaries between investors and financial markets.) *Computerization* refers to the expanding role of electronic systems in the gathering and dissemination of information about financial events, the linking together of widely separate exchanges, and the support of trading in stocks, bonds, and other financial instruments in ways that do not depend on the physical presence of traders on an exchange floor. And finally there is *securitization*: the tendency of capital to be treated not simply as a value-holder making it easier to buy and sell goods and services, but as a commodity in its own right, one that can be bought, sold, speculated in, and packaged in an almost infinite number of ways. The existence of these trends is, of course, significant in itself. But even more important is the degree to which they are inseparable. And it is that very inseparability which, to a great extent, makes the global capital marketplace what it is today.

As the chief executive officer of a major U.S.-based investment firm that is actively participating in this revolution, it is my job to look at where these trends are leading, and to ensure that PaineWebber is well positioned to capitalize on them for the benefit of our customers, our employees, and our stockholders.

My colleagues in some other industries have had a head start in addressing the global marketplace. Since World War II, the market for the fruits of development, from capital goods to consumer products to popular entertainment, has been extended to the remotest corners of the Third World. This process has brought dramatic changes in the health and well-being, the material and cultural life, of people throughout the world. And, at the same time, it has permanently altered the competitive dynamics of industry after industry. There'll be no demurral on this point from the Detroit automaker, the Silicon Valley electronics manufacturer, or the Madison Avenue advertising executive.

Today, that same global market is opening up to the buying and selling of financial services and to the rapid transnational movement of the very lifeblood of economic development—capital itself. This is indeed a fundamental change in economic history, with a potential impact no less significant than the stirring of commerce and the ferment in international affairs that came in the wake of the Age of Exploration. The globalization of capital markets, in increasing opportunities for putting money to work around the world and offering the potential of a greater abundance of goods, services, and jobs, creates the prospect of a rising global standard of living and a greater balance of wealth between today's haves and have-nots. More than this, political and cultural progress should accompany the economic advance: freedom and democratic values go hand in hand with the emergence of a global capital market.

The opportunities for the individual investment firm in this new world parallel the macroeconomic ones. Expanded geographical reach, broadened and enhanced services to clients, new career paths for employees, and increased profitabilty are the rewards of successful participation in the global financial revolution.

Reward does not come without risk—for the world economy at large, or for any individual investment firm. As we'll see later on, the existence of a capital marketplace characterized by globalization, deregulation computerization, and securitization, may actually increase the chances that a financial crisis in one sector of the world economy will have serious repercussions in may others.

But in my judgment, the risks inherent in a global capital

market are outweighed by the rewards. And all of us—from individuals to investment firms to entire nations—have good reason to expect continuing and increasing benefits from the freedom we have to pursue a wide range of investment opportunities wherever they may develop around the world.

FROM BRETTON WOODS TO
THE BIG BANG

History, one might say, is the intersection of trends and events. It is thus possible to trace the roots of the global capital market both in the trends I have mentioned and in a number of specific occurrences.

One of these was the Bretton Woods Conference of 1944, which was attended by the major Western industrial powers and resulted in an international economic system based on free trade and the convertibility of currencies at fixed rates of exchange. Bretton Woods established the International Monetary Fund as a mechanism to help member countries cope with any short-term monetary difficulties. It established the dollar as the world's major reserve currency, and thus the U.S. government as the world's "economic policeman" and lender of last resort. Bretton Woods served the global economy well for thirty years, creating—along with the Marshall Plan—a sense of Europe as a whole and the economic climate necessary for its reconstruction.

Another was the creation of a pool of expatriated U.S. dollars in what has been known since the end of World War II as the Eurodollar market. In the Cold War atmosphere of the 1950s, many Eastern bloc countries, understandably reluctant to deposit their dollars in banks within the United States, opted to keep their dollar-denominated assets in European banks. Other dollars migrated to Europe as a natural result of the continent's economic recovery.

The Eurodollar market really took off, however, less as a consequence of European than of American factors. One of these—and arguably the most important—was the Interest Equalization Tax (IET) passed in 1963, which imposed a 15 percent levy on foreign borrowings in U.S. capital markets.

Another was the so-called Voluntary Foreign Credit Restraint Program of 1965, which limited foreign lending by American banks from their U.S.-based offices. And in 1968, President Johnson demanded that American companies with foreign operations should fund them with foreign borrowings. Other regulations limited the interest banks could pay on savings and other time deposits, and required banks to set aside a substantial portion of their funds in non-interest-bearing accounts.

Whatever the intent of these measures (most were aimed at reducing the U.S. balance-of-payments deficit or otherwise assuring fiscal stability), their effect was to encourage holders of U.S. dollars to keep them—or take them—out of the country and into the relatively untaxed and unregulated Eurodollar market.

The next growth spurt began in 1971, when the Federal government abolished exchange controls and shifted from fixed to floating currency exchange rates. That decision was aimed at discouraging transnational money flows by bringing the world's major currencies more nearly into balance. But again, its primary effect was not the one anticipated: instead of slowing down, transborder flows increased substantially, as banks, corporations, and other institutions took full advantage of their new freedom to lend and borrow abroad and to move their funds wherever and whenever investment opportunities developed.

The most cataclysmic economic event of the 1970s was the rise of OPEC, the cartel of oil-exporting countries that precipitated the oil shocks of 1973 and 1979. Those shocks, whose waves reverberated across the world's financial system, caused a quadrupling of oil prices that provided OPEC members with an extra $150 billion a year—vastly more than the oil producers' home economies could absorb. Much of that "homeless" money thus ended up on deposit in U.S. commercial banks, which recycled the windfall by joining together to make huge "syndicated" loans to Latin America and elsewhere in the Third World.

Yet another significant event, or continuum of events, was the deficit-driven inflation of the late 1970s, which made banks and institutional investors (pension funds, mutual funds, insurance companies, etc.) almost desperate to find outlets for their capital that would preserve its value, regardless of country, currency, or market.

All of these factors contributed to the spectacular growth of the Eurodollar market, and specifically of the market for Eurobonds—80 percent of which were dollar-denominated. (Eurobonds are also issued in such currencies as West German marks, Japanese yen, European Currency Units, Dutch guilders, French francs, and Canadian Australian, or New Zealand dollars.) Between 1966 and 1980, the Eurobond market grew from $17.4 billion to $575 billion, a rate of increase averaging 28.4 percent a year. New Eurobond issues rose from $47.9 billion in 1983 to $133.4 billion in 1985. Eurobonds issued by American corporations increased from $7 billion in 1983 to $35 billion in 1986. The volume of Eurobond issues outstanding is now put at $3 trillion. After U.S. and U.K. government bonds (the latter known as "gilts"), Eurobonds are the world's third largest fixed-rate market. And for many multinationals and governments, Eurobonds are now the preferred way to raise capital.

The rise of the Eurobond market taught the U.S. government an important lesson: burdensome taxes and regulations, in the absence of exchange controls, tend to drive capital out of the country. And so, beginning in the mid-1970s, the United States began deregulating much of the domestic financial industry in an effort to keep domestic capital at home and to attract capital from abroad. In order to maintain their own attractiveness to capital, many other nations soon began to do likewise.

In the United States, a year after the IET was effectively dismantled, came a watershed deregulatory event: "May Day"—May 1, 1975—on which Wall Street abolished fixed commissions on stock market transactions. Among early results of the arrival of price competition on Wall Street were the average 60 percent drop in commission charges paid by institutional investors and the average 20 percent drop in commissions paid by smaller investors. Longer-term consequences included a shakeout of medium-sized securities firms and the merger or acquisition of several others: the acquisition by American Express of Shearson Loeb Rhoades (1981) and of Lehman Brothers (1984); the purchase by Prudential Insurance of Bache Halsey Stuart Shields (1981) to form Prudential-Bache

Securities; Sears Roebuck's acquisition of Dean Witter (1981); Phibro Corporation's purchase of Salomon Brothers (1981); Equitable Life's purchase of Donaldson, Lufkin and Jenrette (1984); General Electric's acquisition of Kidder Peabody (1986). My own firm, PaineWebber, acquired Mitchell Hutchins in 1977, Blyth Eastman Dillon in 1980, Rotan Mosle in 1983, and First MidAmerica in the same year. Additional mergers and acquisitions occurred in the aftermath of the October 1987 crash.

Congress climbed aboard the deregulatory bandwagon in 1980, when it passed the Depository Institutions Deregulation and Money Control Act and thereby abolished Regulation Q—the Federal Reserve Board ceiling on the interest rates banks and other savings institutions could pay on savings and other time deposits. That was followed, a year later, by a liberalization of the rules governing non-interest-bearing deposits and other banking regulations. And a year after that by SEC adoption of Rule 415, allowing "shelf" registration of U.S. securities, substantially reducing the regulatory delays faced by U.S. corporations in selling new securities, and thus enhancing the U.S. capital market's ability to compete with the Euromarket.

Japan yielded to years of competitive (and political) pressure in 1984, when it joined the U.S. in signing the Yen-Dollar Agreement. That landmark measure reduced the Japanese government's role in setting domestic interest rates, created Japan's first short-term money markets, increased the volume of yen-denominated international loans and commercial paper, and opened the Tokyo Stock Exchange to membership by foreign financial institutions. Also in that year, West Germany, long resistant to the internationalization of its currency, abolished the withholding tax on foreign buyers of domestic and foreign issues of Deutschmark bonds, the first of several German deregulatory moves.

The United Kingdom's answer to May Day was the "Big Bang," which came on October 27, 1986, and included the abolition of fixed commissions on the London Stock Exchange, an end to the distinctions between stock brokering, market making, and banking, and the opening up of Exchange membership to outside institutions. (The U.K. had abolished currency exchange controls in 1979, as had Japan in 1980.) Like May Day, the Big Bang was expected to result in a major upheaval of the British financial industry.

Even France, not known up to now for its openness to deregulation, has begun to consider a relaxation of restrictions on its currency and its markets.

Deregulation is certainly the most important single factor in the development of the global capital market. By allowing capital to move far more freely around the world, it has created an environment in which all nations have a chance to compete for capital—not just the giants. By loosening the governmental grip on investment firms, banks, and other financial industry players, it has encouraged the development of new and innovative financial instruments. And by doing that, it has enabled individual and institutional investors to "customize" their portfolios of equity or debt instruments in ways best suited to their particular needs.

We'll take a look at the "micro" and "macro" sides of the global capital market shortly. But first, let's examine another factor that has significantly impacted the financial world, the increasing role of technology.

THE COMPUTERIZED MARKETPLACE

The use of computers for internal, back-office functions like accounting and word processing is, of course, as common today in the financial sector as in every other. But computers are increasingly assuming a front-office, strategic role in the world of finance, and those organizations that have made the best, most imaginative use of information systems have tended to realize a substantial competitive advantage.

An early and now classic example is NASDAQ, the National Association of Securities Dealers' automated quotation system for trading in over-the-counter (OTC) stocks. NASDAQ debuted in 1971, a network of 20,000 miles of leased telephone lines, dealer-office video terminals, and a central computer. The terminals display information on the average, bid, and asked prices of OTC and even NYSE-listed stocks, allowing dealers actually to enter quotes and make markets on-line—and far from any exchange floor.

The NASDAQ network, enjoying continuing and rapid growth (partly at the expense of the traditional, trading-floor exchanges), now has 158,000 terminals, an average daily trading volume of 114 million shares, and an annual trading volume of 29 billion shares with a total value of $378 billion. It boasts a number of American corporations that would presumably have little difficulty listing on the New York Stock Exchange, and nearly 200 foreign securities as well. A product of deregulation and computerization, NASDAQ may be the model for tomorrow's global, electronic stock exchange.

Another early example of computerized trading is Instinet (from *Inst*itutional *Net*works Corporation), a "Fourth Market" electronic stock exchange enabling participating institutional investors to conduct large block trades among themselves, thereby avoiding brokerage commissions. Over a hundred institutions now subscribe to the fully-automated system, which handled 922 million shares in 1986 and deals in virtually every stock traded on the major exchanges. Today, in addition to U.S. stocks, Instinet quotes foreign stocks and options on stocks and currencies from the Chicago Board Options Exchange. In addition, Instinet has joined Reuters in forming a computerized quote and order service for international stocks.

Other NASDAQ- and Instinet-like approaches include ITS, LIFFE, and Intex. The Intermarket Trading System (ITS), introduced by the New York Stock Exchange in 1978, electronically links the NYSE's specialists with traders in the same securities at the American, Boston, Midwest, Philadelphia, Cincinnati, and Pacific Exchanges, permitting orders to be communicated, but not actually executed, in a national clearing system. LIFFE, the London International Financial Futures Exchange, debuted in 1982, offering institutional investors highly automated quotation and settlement services for that family of financial instruments. Bermuda-based Intex, which opened for business in 1985, supports fully automated trading in gold contracts, U.S. Treasury securities, and freight.

In the opinion of many observers, it is only a matter of time before we see the development of truly 24-hour markets linking together exchanges on different continents and handling a limited number of so-called "world-class" stocks, issued by large, well-managed companies and traded on several exchanges around the world 24 hours a day, seven days a week. For some time, IBM stock has been among several foreign issues traded on the Tokyo Stock Exchange, and several foreign issues, including British Telecommunications and Reuters, are now traded on the New York Stock Exchange.

The beginning of this 24-hour exchange can already be seen in the increasing prevalence of clearing, quotation, and trading links joining various trading centers. In 1984, the Chicago Mercantile Exchange and the Singapore International Monetary Exchange linked up to offer round-the-clock trading in financial futures. In April 1986, a two-year pilot program was launched to establish a quotation link between NASDAQ and the London Stock Exchange. Also in 1986, an experiment began to study the feasibility of a computer linkage between NASDAQ and the $2.2 trillion Eurobond market. And in 1987, the Chicago Merc and Reuters Holdings PLC announced a plan to offer electronically based, off-hours international financial futures and options trading. The main impediment to such international linkages is the absence, so far, of international standards for clearing, settling, disclosure, and surveillance. But the development of such standards, like the development of the 24-hour exchange itself, may just be a matter of time.

The retail banking industry discovered the strategic possibilities of computers in the 1970s, when a few of the larger banks began to install cash dispensers from which customers with magnetic-stripe identification cards could replenish their pocket money. These devices evolved, in the 1980s, into automated teller machines (ATMs), EFTPOS devices (for electronic funds transfer at point of sale), and, most recently, "smart cards" with an embedded microchip that stores the holder's account balance and updates it as debits and credits occur. Indicative of the strategic importance of such electronic devices, financial institutions have already spent considerably more than $2 billion on ATMs, 50,000 of which had been installed in the United States by the end of 1985.

Computers operated by large banks and linked to the most advanced telecommunications systems can be enormously useful to multinational companies maintaining accounts in many different countries and currencies. Each account is likely to earn or pay a different interest rate, making the tasks of monitoring and control daunting without computerized assistance. The banks that can offer those functions are much stronger candidates for the multinationals' business.

Computers are also an integral part of two major international payments systems, the Federal Reserve's Fedwire and the New York Clearing House's Interbank Payments System, CHIPS, which together currently clear an average of $1.1 trillion dollars in domestic interbank, foreign exchange, and Eurodollar transactions daily. Such volumes would be unthinkable without today's high-speed, highly reliable mainframe computer systems.

Also unthinkable without those computers would be many of the financial instruments available today in the global capital market. As the following remarks will indicate, the number, range, and complexity of those instruments have burgeoned in today's deregulated, computerized capital marketplace.

AN EXPLOSION OF CHOICES

Deregulation, industry consolidation, and increasing competition have led some investment firms to become "financial supermarkets" offering everything from credit cards to retail brokerage services to corporate financial services to real estate and insurance. This is not the way PaineWebber has chosen to go: we prefer to focus on a few lines of business in which the quality of service we can offer our clients is second to none. But however many lines of business an individual investment firm pursues, we are all witnessing an explosion in the number of products available to investors, a trend often referred to as securitization.

Available from New York Stock Exchange members alone are more than 200 different investment products. The profusion of products now widely offered includes stocks, straight bonds, zero coupon bonds, convertible bonds, junk bonds, bonds with warrants, subordinated debt, government bond funds, options, swaps, futures, index futures, master limited partnerships, debt-backed securities, and hybrids. The names and nicknames of some instruments are cryptic, even bizarre: CATS, TIGERS, LYONS, sushis, samurais, and shoguns. Many exotic offerings are dreamed up by "rocket scientists" intent, it sometimes seems, less on maximum profit than on maximum complexity. While complaints of "marketing gimmickry" may occasionally be valid, most of the financial instruments available today are worthwhile additions to the financial marketplace, and reflect the genuine needs of borrowers and investors for products that will keep pace with inflation, protect against market volatility, and minimize borrowing costs or maximize return.

There are, of course, far too many instruments available to discuss them all. But three or four in particular deserve a brief description, as they embody the innovation and flexibility that is characteristic of today's global market.

One of the earliest and most important examples of securitization was the floating rate note (FRN), which debuted in the Euromarket in the early 1970s. A major factor in the rise of that market, the FRN is a debt instrument whose yield is lower than fixed rate notes of comparable maturity, but whose rate is adjusted periodically to keep it in line with inflation. According to the Organization for Economic Cooperation and Development, floating rate notes accounted for 23 percent of the $256.5 billion borrowed in international capital markets in 1985, versus 36 percent for traditional straight bonds.

Two other early innovations, bearing a strong resemblance to the traditional standby letter of credit, were the note issuance facility (NIF) and the revolving underwriting facililty (RUF). NIFs and RUFs appeal to borrowers by making it easier for them to issue short-term securities in the Euromarket; that's because the facility is backed by a bank—which commits itself to purchase any notes that can't be sold or to lend a comparable amount. And they appeal to banks because they generate fees whether they are drawn down or not, and because they don't appear on the issuing bank's balance sheet, hence don't tie up its capital. Reflecting the popularity of these securitized instruments, the NIF market has grown tenfold in the past two years, and now stands at $75 billion.

Today's globalized financial environment has made possible

another novel instrument, the swap, which has made it considerably easier for companies to raise money around the world. There are two varieties here: the interest rate swap and the currency swap. The former involves the exchange by two companies of their respective interest payments, usually one of them floating and the other fixed. The latter involves an agreement to exchange quantities of one currency for those of another.

Swaps, which first appeared internationally only a few years ago, have become an increasingly important part of Euromarket activity. Between 1983 and 1984 they tripled in volume, with new interest rate swaps totaling $65 billion and new currency swaps as much as $15 billion. In the fourth quarter of 1985 alone, completed interest rate swaps totaled $36 billion. Swaps were involved in an estimated 60 percent of 1985 international capital market issues. The cumulative total of $170 billion in 1985, and $313 billion in 1986, also supported a large secondary market. Swaps are especially appealing to commercial banks, which have the international connections and the relationships with multinational corporations that make it relatively easy for them to find partners and to serve them as an intermediary, for a fee.

That is a brief glimpse of the "micro" side of the picture—the level of securitized products. Let's look now at the "macro" side, to get an idea of the kind of world deregulation, computerization, and securitization have created.

A GLOBALIZED ECONOMY

To begin with, ours is a world increasingly defined by the activities of three principal trading centers: New York, London, and Tokyo.

New York, of course, has Wall Street, the great New York Stock Exchange, the headquarters of the world's now-second largest bank in terms of assets (Citicorp), and a host of other major financial institutions.

London has the world's second largest stock exchange and is the undisputed capital of currency, commodity, and Eurobond trading. Despite its shrinking domestic economic base, the U.K. still has many of the world's top corporations, commercial and merchant banks, insurance companies and pension funds.

Tokyo has the world's largest bank in terms of assets—Dai-Ichi Kangyo, which displaced Citicorp from the top spot in 1986—seven of the top ten in terms of capital, and five of the ten largest securities and financial services firms ranked by capital. In early 1987, the Tokyo stock exchange, with nearly $3 trillion in market capitalization, became the world's largest in this respect. Japan's capital outflows total more than $40 billion a year. Its 1986 GNP of $2.2 trillion was second only to that of the U.S. And now that deregulation is taking hold in Japan as it has in other major financial capitals, we can expect the Japanese to play as central a role in the world of global finance as the Japanese consumer electronics and automobile industries did in their respective industry sectors.

It's a world in which institutional investors are increasingly prominent. Changes in U.S. pension laws a decade ago made it easier for pension funds to build up large capital resources. As a result, institutions typically account for more than 50 percent of daily trading on the New York Stock Exchange, and sometimes 70 percent or more. Institutions in the U.S. and overseas today hold 44 percent of the market value of U.S. stocks, four times more than 35 years ago. One survey showed that the 200 largest pension funds held assets of just over $1 trillion as of September 1986, $440 billion of which was invested in stock.

It's a world of enormous numbers, in part because deregulation, computerization, and the abandonment of exchange controls make it possible to move large sums of money between nations, markets, and financial instruments at the speed of light and as often as market conditions dictate. Today, for example, the U.S. commercial paper market (commercial paper being short-term obligations issued by banks, corporations, and other borrowers to investors with temporarily idle funds) totals $300 billion, versus $35 billion only five years ago. On most days, $200 billion worth of foreign exchange is traded worldwide, more than twice the volume of five years ago. Only a tenth of that amount represents currency corporations need to pay for goods purchased and services rendered abroad. The other 90 percent represents trading for profit only. The total volume of U.S. transactions is now more than $1 trillion *a day*, one-third of the entire gross national product. Trades involving U.S. government securities alone total nearly $30 trillion annually—dwarfing not only the GNP but the national debt and even the nation's assessed value.

It's a world of dramatic changes in global economics. Not many years ago, the United States was the world's biggest creditor; it is now the world's biggest debtor. A decade ago, the largest river of capital ran from the Middle East to South America by way of the United States; today, the flow is from Japan and it terminates in the U.S.

It's a world of growing U.S. investment abroad, and of growing foreign investment in the United States. According to the Securities Industry Association, U.S. net purchases of foreign stocks totaled a record $3.9 billion in 1985, then soared to $2.1 billion in the first quarter of 1986 alone. Americans made net purchases of $1.1 billion in Japanese stocks, also increasing their holdings of British, French, and German equities. According to the Commerce Department, the net inflow of foreign funds totaled $117.4 billion in 1986 and $303.7 billion between 1982 and 1986.

Foreign investment in U.S. stock began accelerating in the early 1980s, as a consequence of the higher growth rate of this country as compared to Europe or Japan. The bull market that began on Wall Street in 1982—and that ended abruptly on October 19, 1987—set many records: for example, foreign net purchases of U.S. stock in the first quarter of 1986 came to $6.4 billion, more than the total of any previous entire year. The 1986 total was $18.5 billion, triple the previous record set in 1983. What made this all the more impressive was that the dollar fell nearly 30 percent between early 1985 and mid-1986, and, moreover, that both the Tokyo and the London stock exchanges outperformed Wall Street during the same period. Foreign trading in U.S. stocks totaled well over $200 billion in 1987.

Who is buying all that stock? Europeans, mostly: $4.8 billion of net stock purchases in the first quarter of 1986; and British and Swiss investors for $3.7 billion of that. The British, and particularly U.K. pension fund managers, led European investment in U.S. equities.

According to a recent study by the National Association of Securities Dealers, U.S. brokerage firms now have more than 250 branches in 32 foreign countries, and more than 110 foreign investment firms have located in the United States.

Foreign investors continue to be drawn to U.S. government securities and corporate bonds as well. They hold 20 percent of U.S. government securities and, according to the Commerce Department, held $42 billion in corporate bonds in 1986, up from $32.8 billion in 1984.

The leading purchasers of both Treasury and corporate bonds are the Japanese. With its high rate of personal saving (22 percent, versus 5 percent in the U.S.) and huge institutional resources, Japan is now the largest net buyer of U.S. government securities, purchasing an additional $10 billion each month. It currently holds more than 20 percent of total U.S. debt, and in some months has bought as much as 40 percent of new Treasury bond issues. Japanese banks now hold more international assets than do those of any other country, including the United States. Practically all these assets—a total of $640 billion—are dollar-denominated.

An increasing number of U.S. corporations are looking overseas not just for markets in which to sell their goods but for ways to meet their financial needs, through the sale of stock or the issuance of bonds. According to a recent Conference Board study, the reasons most often given by management for international financings are cost-effectiveness and the expansion of funding sources. Others include the opportunity to obtain arbitrage profits; less restrictive borrowing covenants; the desire to hedge overseas assets; freedom from domestic regulatory restraints; term, tax, and foreign exchange considerations; easier, less voluminous, documentation for issues; and the favorable publicity that may result from an overseas debt offering, which in turn can lead to increased demand for the company's stock.

Deregulation and disintermediation have contributed to a shakeout of the U.S. banking industry. Between 1981 and 1985, corporate and sovereign bonds issued internationally rose fourfold, to $162.8 billion, but internationally syndicated bank loans fell to $21.6 billion from $96.5 billion as corporations found it cheaper to issue traditional debt securities than to borrow from banks. During the same period, some 1,000 U.S. thrifts—25 percent of all such institutions—disappeared or were merged after struggling to finance mortgages and other fixed-rate loans with floating-rate deposits. As of late 1987, there were approximately 1,600 commercial banks on the Federal Deposit Insurance Corporation's problem list, more than one out of every ten such institutions.

INFORMATION, STANDARDS, AND RELATIONSHIPS

For the investment banker who is thinking of underwriting a new issue, offering a new product, or entering a new market in this high-stakes, highly dynamic environment, accurate and timely information about the competitive and regulatory landscape is absolutely essential. Like an automaker planning to bring out a new kind of car, the banker must consider the current size of a market sector, its prospects for future growth, the strengths and weaknesses of his competitors, and the way each has positioned itself. Understanding all this in a metropolitan, regional, or national context is complicated enough. But doing so in a global environment is a great deal more challenging. The valuation of a nation's currency, for example, reflects not only trading patterns but macroeconomic patterns, which may be out of synch with international realities.

Traditionally, brokerage firms have employed teams of analysts who track developments and project earnings at particular companies as a basis for stock buy/sell recommendations. But today, when anything that happens in one market is likely to be reflected rapidly in others, the framework of analysis has broadened considerably. Whenever an international crisis develops, a national election is called, or an important economic statistic is released, traders worldwide at once begin to analyze the ramifications and trade accordingly.

One important area for analysis is the intrinsic stability of a given market, and that, to a great extent, is a question of standards. In a global market where capital is free to go anywhere, markets that do not run smoothly and predictably will tend to be avoided. That fact is a great force for good behavior in nations and markets all over the world.

Investment firms' increasingly voracious appetite for information has led to a dramatic rise in the costs associated with obtaining it. The communications network and computer systems needed to gather and process mountains of data may require tens of millions of dollars to install and maintain; the analysts and technical personnel needed for a large-scale research operation, millions more.

In addition, competitive pressures among investment firms have been intensifying, encouraging some to participate in securities offerings not just as advisors but as principals. For these and other reasons, the capital needs of investment firms have grown enormously, leading to many mergers with cash-rich corporations and a widespread tendency to seek safety in bigness.

But bigness is neither necessary nor sufficient. Notwithstanding the huge numbers involved in some deals, the technology on which so many instruments depend, and the complexity of many product lines, one of the most important components of successful investment banking is still the quality of human relationships.

May Day, the Big Bang, and other deregulatory developments tended to break down many banker-client relationships. In the pre-deregulation era, it didn't much matter which firm a client used from the standpoint of price, since all firms charged the same amount. So clients went with the firms that employed friends, neighbors, or college classmates. Deregulation changed all that by encouraging clients to do business with the firm—or firms—offering the best price.

But the fact is that investment banking is still a people business. Relationships still matter—and arguably matter more than ever. Not relationships based on social ties as before, but rather based on the timeliness and accuracy of the information and analysis a good investment banker and his firm can provide. In that regard, I'm pleased to say that my own firm, though not the largest investment house in the business today, is nevertheless an industry leader.

A PAINEWEBBER PROFILE

Securities firms have been responding to the trends I've been discussing by becoming more active in the global marketplace. Let's take a look at my own firm, PaineWebber, as an example of those four trends in action.

PaineWebber, whose 1987 revenues were a record $2.44 billion and whose capitalization now exceeds $1.4 billion, has four core businesses—Retail Sales, Capital Transactions, Asset Management and Banking. Each business actively deals with those trends in ways intended to achieve maximum benefit for our clients and shareholders.

Retail Sales consists primarily of a domestic branch office system and consumer product groups through which the firm provides investment products and brokerage services to individual clients. The number and variety of these products, which include equities, bonds, money market instruments, options, futures, mutual funds, annuities, and direct investments, reflect the richness of the current financial environment. Supplemented by regular and special research and market reports as well as customized advice, they enable PaineWebber's customers to tailor their portfolios to best meet their particular investment objectives. Recognizing a flight-to-quality trend among the investment public, PaineWebber's new product offerings emphasize the value of diversification and professional management.

Capital Transactions includes the company's Institutional Equity, Fixed Income, and High Yield divisions, and PaineWebber International. PaineWebber allocates resources to those trading businesses where the firm has an opportunity to become or remain a leading competitor in the global market. These include U.S. government securities, mortgages, listed and over-the-counter equities and their derivative products. Supporting these trading capabilities are strong institutional sales efforts that provide integrated service to leading domestic and international clients. In the Institutional Equity sales and trading business, PaineWebber is one of Wall Street's leaders. The division takes positions in both listed and unlisted equity securities to facilitate client transactions, for the company's own account, or in connection with arbitrage activities. In institutional sales, the company places securities with, and executes trades on behalf of, institutional clients. Working with PaineWebber International, Institutional Equity has established a convertible trading desk in London, enhancing the firm's position in the global marketplace.

In the sales and trading of Fixed Income securities, Paine-Webber has a proven record of successful risk management and a continuing emphasis on innovative client services. With a solid presence in London and Tokyo, the firm continues to build a strong foothold in the global markets. Additionally, PaineWebber Incorporated is a primary dealer in U.S. government, government-guaranteed and agency securities. The firm also underwrites, sells, and trades municipal securities. PaineWebber's High Yield unit structures and arranges financing for large mergers and acquisitions and leveraged transactions.

The *Asset Management* group is composed of Mitchell Hutchins Asset Management and PaineWebber Properties Incorporated. The former provides investment advisory and portfolio management services to individuals, pension and endowment funds, and mutual funds. The latter originates and manages real estate investment partnerships.

Since entering the mutual funds business in 1984, PaineWebber has brought 19 open-ended funds and several closed-end funds to market, all managed by Mitchell Hutchins Asset Management. Three of the latter—the Atlas, Master Global Income, and Master Energy-Utility funds—are global funds, designed to help individual investors benefit from worldwide investment opportunities. In addition to providing investors with access to professional management and diversified risk, the mutual funds business provides the firm with revenue streams from advisory fees that are less susceptible to market cycles.

PaineWebber Properties is continuing to diversify its client base to include institutional and foreign investors, who are showing renewed investor interest in real estate as a result of securities market volatility.

PaineWebber International has offices in New York, London, Paris, Zurich, Geneva, Athens, Tokyo, Hong Kong, San Juan, and Miami. It provides institutional and retail brokerage services, investment banking services, underwriting and private placement facilities, Eurodollar securities and foreign exchange trading, and private banking for the company's international clients. PaineWebber International also gives domestic clients access to the global capital markets.

In 1987, PaineWebber International showed continued growth in institutional equity sales and made significant gains in its international futures and foreign exchange businesses. A New York sales and trading desk for futures, options, and foreign exchange was established to complement existing activities in London and Hong Kong. As a result, Paine-Webber's international clients now have 24-hour access to these markets.

The establishment of PaineWebber International Bank Ltd. in London and the introduction in 1987 of the International Resource Management Account for non-U.S. residents give the firm the vehicles to provide a full range of investment products and services to offshore high net worth individuals.

Having carefully controlled the firm's global expansion over the last few years, PaineWebber International is now taking advantage of selected growth opportunities. For example, the firm increased its professional staff in Puerto Rico by 30 percent in 1987, laying the foundation to further increase market share. In 1988, PaineWebber International will open offices in Lugano, Monte Carlo, Milan, and Munich, to serve individual and institutional clients in these markets.

In *banking*, PaineWebber's dual focus is on high-margin products and strong long-term client relationships. The firm also remains willing to commit capital to merchant banking activities. Through the banking group, PaineWebber provides financial advice to, and raises capital for, a broad range of corporate clients. The investment banking division manages and underwrites public offerings, privately places debt and equity securities and provides advice in connection with mergers and acquisitions and lease financings. Through

PaineWebber Capital Inc., the company conducts merchant banking activities and arranges and participates in research and development financing.

The banking group focuses on key product areas (mergers and acquisitions, private placements, leveraged transactions, and public equity offerings) and on target client industries (transportation, industrial/emerging growth, financial services, and communications.

Lower stock prices resulting from the October 1987 crash, and the depressed value of the dollar, are making U.S. companies more attractive to foreign investors, especially those in the U.K. and Far East, resulting in increased cross-border investment banking opportunities. Thus, an Asian investment banking group formed during 1987 assisted in Japanese debt and lease transactions for new transportation clients in the Far East.

The firm's international investment banking unit expanded its staff in the cross border mergers and acquisitions area in London, thereby enabling PaineWebber to service European companies more effectively. The firm continues to play an active role in the arrangement of syndicated loan and note issuance facilities. PaineWebber bankers have also increased the firm's volume of offshore financing for airlines, utilities, and government authorities.

Research and Technology. Strong support systems are essential for the success of the firm's core business. In addition to its well-respected coverage of domestic companies and industries, PaineWebber's Research division began offering integrated global research in 1987, introducing both a proprietary Global Asset Allocation model for investment strategy, and a European Research team to cover international companies in conjunction with the domestic research teams. In all, this highly respected division covers more than 725 companies.

Since 1985, PaineWebber has also made a significant commitment to improved technology, including construction of a state-of-the-art Data Center in Lincoln Harbor, New Jersey. Completion of this project in 1987 gave PaineWebber the most efficient support environment in the securities industry, with the technology necessary to take the firm into the next century.

With a technology platform that includes two IBM 3090 mainframes, the data center proved an invaluable asset during the turbulent days of late October 1987, when PaineWebber's technology successfully met the challenge of unprecedented daily stock-exchange volume with no interruptions of service other than those created by external factors.

As the growth of sophisticated financial products and services accelerates, and as global market volatility remains a fact of life for the industry, investment firms' operations, including computer systems, play an increasingly pivotal role in shaping competitive advantage.

The Yasuda Partnership. In 1987, PaineWebber accelerated its pace of global expansion by making a strategic alliance with a partner who would not only strengthen the firm's capital base but also introduce PaineWebber to new foreign business opportunities in the Far East, particularly Japan. In November 1987, PaineWebber signed a definitive agreement with the Yasuda Mutual Life Insurance Company, Japan's fifth largest issuer of life insurance and a member of the influential Fuyo Group, a coalition of 29 leading Japanese corporations. Yasuda subsequently made a $300 million equity investment in PaineWebber—in exchange for approximately 6.7 million shares of 7 percent Cumulative Convertible Exchangeable Voting Preferred Stock, Series A—another indication of the growing ties linking every corner of the global capital market.

RISKS AND REWARDS

It has often been noted that the globalization of capital carries with it a number of significant risks. Let's take a look at some of them.

The risk most on everyone's mind—and properly so in light of the near "market meltdown" of October 19-20, 1987—is that the collapse of one market, exchange, or financial institution could set off a "chain reaction" liquidity crisis taking the rest of the world's financial system with it. This risk is increased, in the view of some, by the fact that all of the world's major markets are now linked electronically. Some older members of the financial community can still recall the events that triggered the Great Depression: a bank failure in Austria, followed by the devaluation of the British pound, leading in turn to the collapse of the whole, unsuspectedly fragile financial establishment.

How could such a "chain reaction" crisis occur today? According to one scenario, it could be triggered by the failure of a major commercial bank, brought on by a default on one or more of its syndicated loans.

In theory, syndicated lending—in which groups of commercial banks co-manage large loans to corporate or sovereign borrowers—spreads risk so widely that each bank's exposure is tolerable. But it is possible that the spreading of risk also diffuses responsibility, so that the total risk is actually increased. The number of syndicated loans to the Third World that are now in arrears or that have had to be rescheduled suggests that the standards applied in syndication situations may not be quite as high as loans made on a one-to-one basis.

Another risk factor cited—and widely implicated in the October 1987 crash—is the widespread use of swaps, futures, and options as hedges. For example, if one party in a swap arrangement defaults on his part of the agreement, he could drag the counterparty down as well; and that counterparty's failure could trigger other failures down the line.

It's important to remember that swaps, futures, options, and other hedges don't reduce risk; they only transfer it. Nor are they foolproof. For example, futures contracts on government securities are often used as a hedge in conjunction with mortgage-backed securities, on the usually valid assumption that they will move in opposite directions. But in 1986, a drop in interest rates disrupted the usual relationship between mortgage-backed and government securities and cost securities firms a half billion dollars.

As noted earlier, NIFs, RUFs, and similar securitized instruments are attractive to banks because they enable banks to reduce their assets (loans) subject to regulation and increase the funds they have available to seek out new growth opportunities. The danger here is that by removing from their balance sheets some of their most solid assets—loans to dependable customers who provide them with steady income in the form of interest payments—the banks are left with assets of less obvious quality: sovereign debt to the Third World or loans to declining industries. Ironically, by pursuing this strategy, banks may actually improve their capital-asset ratio, and thus mask their increased exposure. There is no guarantee, moreover, that the growth opportunities banks discern in the capital marketplace will ever pan out.

So far, only 20 percent of NIFs have actually been drawn down. But a panic set off by a sudden rise in interest rates or a major corporate failure could conceivably make it difficult for even healthy companies to borrow in the commercial paper market, and thereby set off a liquidity crisis among NIF- and RUF-issuing banks.

In response to this danger, the regulators of some countries are requiring banks to increase their reserves. Between 1982 and 1985, according to the Federal Reserve, primary capital at fifty of the largest U.S. bank holding companies rose 68 percent, versus an asset increase of 27 percent. Recently, bankers in the U.K., West Germany, and the Netherlands have been required to include some of their off-balance sheet exposure in calculating their capital-adequacy ratios, a possibility also being considered in the U.S. and Japan.

Another fear is that globalization in all of its manifestations will overwhelm the surveillance systems now in place at the world's major exchanges. According to Don Solodar, Senior Vice President for market surveillance services at the New York Stock Exchange, even state-of-the-art computer systems may soon not be equal to the task of keeping track of the exchange. Says Solodar: "Five years from now, even with automation, we could well be behind the eight ball again because of internationalization. I would suspect that you're going to have more and more types of people coming into the industry who weren't there before. We're going to have more firms, more registered reps, more banks coming into our business. In order for the system to continue working, member firms will have to want to take on more responsibility for self-regulation." The recent insider trading scandals suggest that in some respects, the financial industry may already be behind the eightball with regard to self-regulation.

Deregulation is widely viewed as a prerequisite to success in the financial, as in many other, spheres. But as Walter Wriston noted not long ago, a corollary of the freedom to succeed is the freedom to fail. And unlike some industries, a major failure in the financial sector could, to be sure, have far-reaching consequences. Moreover, the near-meltdown of October 1987 was a warning to those financial services firms whose "strategy" was to be all things to all people, a reminder, to those who needed reminding, that this is a cyclical, often unpredictable business in which prices can go down as well as up, and in which those who become greedy or reckless can get badly burned. Nevertheless, the advantages of a deregulated, computerized, securitized global capital marketplace, it seems to me, clearly offset the risks.

Deregulation, as we've seen, removes artificial barriers to the flow of capital, encourages the development of new financial instruments, and thus gives investors more to choose from in building their portfolios. Computerization streamlines the operations of markets, enables widely separate markets to function as one, and thereby increases overall market efficiency. The use of computers in strategic applications can win new business. And computers handle the complex calculations underlying many of today's financial instruments. Securitization helps banks, corporations, and individual investors protect against volatile shifts in interest rates and exchange rates. It increases the liquidity of assets, making them easier to buy and sell. It gives investors access to previously unavailable assets, such as securities based on mortgages, automobile loans, or credit card debt. It can spread the risk of bond financing among many investors rather than confining it to the banking system.

Globalization is a powerful way to promulgate American values, prominent among which is the free enterprise system we call capitalism. There are few ideas more compelling than that of buying a stock at ten and selling it at twenty.

The globalization of capital also provides the family of nations with a peaceful way of redistributing the world's wealth. History makes it clear that resdistribution will take place one way or another, often by far less civilized means than international trade and economic competition. The globalization of capital provides, in short, an opportunity to build international interdependence, understanding, and trust; to increase worldwide employment; to foster economic growth; and to build a global economic infrastructure that can improve the outlook for international prosperity and lasting peace.

Dr. Karlheinz Kaske

Dr. Karlheinz Kaske, president and chief executive officer of Siemens AG, succeeded Dr. Bernhard Plettner in this position in January 1981. Dr. Kaske had been deputy chairman of the managing board since 1980 and a member of the managing board since 1975.

Dr. Kaske studied physics in Danzig and Aachen before joining Siemens & Halske AG in 1950, where he was engaged in research and development activities at the former Werner Works for measurement technology in Karlsruhe. He left Siemens from 1953 to 1960 to work for the Association of Coalmining Industries in Aachen, where he also served on the faculty of the mining school. Dr. Kaske returned to Siemens in 1963 to head the sales division for automation of power plants.

In 1967, Dr. Kaske became an advisor for Fuji Electric Co. Ltd. in Tokyo. A year later, he joined a planning group and helped draft a new organizational plan for Siemens companies.

Dr. Kaske was head of the Motor Work in Nürnberg from 1969 to 1973, and was promoted to head the Measurement and Process Technology operation in 1973. From 1977 until 1980, he headed the Power Engineering Group.

3
ORGANIZING FOR
AND MEETING
THE GLOBAL CHALLENGE

Dr. Karlheinz Kaske
President and Chief Executive Officer
Siemens AG, Federal Republic of Germany

INTERNATIONAL ROOTS AND
GLOBAL OUTLOOK

From its very beginnings, the Siemens organization has been international in outlook. In 1847 when Werner Siemens formed a company in Berlin to manufacture telegraph equipment and cables, he envisioned the use of this equipment to communicate across national borders and even continents. And his vision soon became a reality.

Throughout the 19th century, the global flavor of the company continued to develop. In the 1860s, two of Werner Siemens' brothers, Carl and Friedrich Siemens, established businesses in Petersburg (now Leningrad) and London. During the next decade, Siemens was involved in laying the first transatlantic cable. The ship *Faraday*, designed and owned by Siemens, completed the link between Ireland and Rhode Island in 1875. By 1884, the ship had been used to lay five additional transatlantic cables.

Other examples of the company's disposition toward international opportunities include an 1881 meeting with Thomas Edison, a cooperative discourse that led to the manufacture of filament lamps by Siemens for European markets; and the opening of offices in Chicago and, later, New York City.

Today, Siemens is one of the world's largest electrical and electronic companies. Headquartered in Munich, we employ more than 359,000 people in 127 countries. Sales reached DM 51 billion during the last fiscal year (about $31 billion based on an exchange rate of 1.68 DM/$1).

The company is organized into seven operating and five central administration and service groups. The operating groups, each with its own worldwide manufacturing, marketing and development operations, are: Communications and Information Systems, Medical Engineering, Telecommunications Networks and Security Systems, Components, Energy and Automation Technology, Installation and Automotive Technology, and the newly integrated KWU (power generation and transmission) group.

Operations of this scope and magnitude, and the economic growth they foster worldwide, could not have been built in a highly restrictive international economic environment. Liberal access to the established and emerging markets of the world during the post World War II era had to have existed.

The recognition of the close connection between free trade and the growth of prosperity is nothing new. Classic economists such as as Adam Smith observed this correlation, and proved it conclusively. Nevertheless, it took almost two centuries for these proofs regarding the positive effect of international trade to be accepted.

The gradual elimination of trade barriers that began after World War II produced soaring growth rates in world trade, rates which were much higher than the increase in the gross domestic product of the world as a whole. The resulting intensification of trade relations created a strong impetus for growth.

Without this opening up of markets, prosperity within participating countries would never have developed so rapidly. The countries that are most integrated in the world market are often the fastest-growing as well, and this is one reason the continued liberalization of trade regulations is so necessary if the world economy is to grow and prosper.

Europe, for example, is still far from being a genuine homogeneous, integrated market. The governments of the EC member countries are aware of this fact. By signing the Single European Act in 1986, they agreed to work to make this integrated market a reality by 1992.

The magnitude and difficulty of this task becomes obvious when you look at the approximately 300 reconciliation areas that must be approached. These issues include not only border controls and the elimination of technical obstacles to trade, but also public procurement, a uniform market for services, general requirements for the capital market and corporate cooperation, the protection of intellectual property, and the elimination of tax barriers.

Siemens will continue to work toward an integrated European and world economy. It is our belief that trade restrictions, despite their short-term appeal, can only bring harm in the longer term. Companies, and nations, must eventually face the hard realities of economic life. They must work to improve their lot through productivity and quality increases, not legislation. Economics has, and always will prevail, over protectionist stopgaps.

ELECTRONICS IN THE INTERNATIONAL ARENA

Whatever is true of the world market as a whole also applies to the worldwide electrical and electronics market in which Siemens participates. In fact, international trade in electrical and electronics has expanded at a faster rate than world trade in general.

As Siemens prepares to enter the 1990s, world trade—the global challenge, particularly in our markets—has become much more complex than Adam Smith or even the authors of postwar recovery might have imagined. Social and political considerations rank more equally than ever with economic tactics, and market approaches vary widely depending on the product and the characteristics of the market concerned.

Let's look at the types of international competition in which Siemens, at least, engages. For us, the word "global" can mean two things from a business point of view.

We can talk about global products/services—in other words, products and services that are sold the world over irrespective of national markets and preferences. An example within Siemens is electronic components—the microchip—at least when it is a commodity. This is a heavily-populated marketplace filled with many international contenders. Other examples could be personal computers or electric motors.

On the other hand, we can look at competition on a global scale in which a relatively small number of companies possessing the required technological, human and financial resources compete in highly specialized, selective markets.

One example of this highly focused worldwide activity in our spectrum is central office telephone switches. Tremendous research and development expenditures are required if a company wants to keep up with the competition from a technological point of view in a market such as this. The same holds true for electric power generation systems and facilities.

These large expenditures can only be recaptured by firms with correspondingly large sales volumes and market shares. In fact, it is estimated that at this time only six or seven companies in the world are large enough to survive in the arena of public switching. A minimum 10 percent market share is clearly required. Market shares approaching 15 percent may be needed in the years ahead.

In either case, the competition is on a global scale, a fact that will certainly lessen the influence of national borders. In turn, the home market takes on considerably less importance.

The global challenge, then, can take many forms. It can be the challenge of worldwide competition with many competitors in specific product areas, or it can be competition with the few competitors capable of projecting many or all of their businesses on a global scale. In the long run, only a company in the forefront of technological progress will be successful in the search for new markets and new sales opportunities. This has led to a steady intensification of technological competition, with the result that innovation cycles are getting shorter and shorter. In the past, 10 to 15 years went by before old products were replaced by new ones in our industry. Now, it takes only four or five years.

The acceleration of the race for new technology, with higher research and development costs, and a similarly rapid increase in capital expenditures for production facilities, have brought about new economic developments. Perhaps the most important of these is the intensifying process of international concentration and cooperation. This wave of international mergers and joint ventures conceal technological and economic pressures that cannot be eliminated by legislation.

The toughening-up process of global competition over the last decades was a major prerequisite for the big economic successes of the subsequent decades, particularly in the export business. Free competition and the opening up of domestic markets forced companies such as Siemens to be constantly on the lookout for new sales opportunities.

The Siemens "home" market in the Federal Republic of Germany is not very big—accounting as it does for only about 6 percent of the total world market for industrial goods. Therefore, the company was forced, from the very beginning, to be increasingly aware of the markets beyond its home base—at least more so than American and Japanese companies, whose domestic markets are considerably larger.

FACING THE GLOBAL CHALLENGE

How does Siemens try to cope with the global challenge? First of all, not all Siemens business is global in scope. In a number of areas, our operations are still restricted to certain parts of the globe.

More than 70 percent of our sales are achieved in European countries. Add to this about 10 percent of our sales gained from the United States, and you get 80 percent of our business coming from Western Europe and the United States and only 20 percent from the rest of the world.

The significance of this is readily apparent. Europe represents a mature market for Siemens and the United States represents a market in which we are seeking to grow a Siemens presence. But the rest of the world represents markets where we must position ourselves as an active and contributory partner.

We must confront this global challenge if we are to overcome the image of being a European company with a North American presence. The question, then, really is how to respond to this global challenge. What must be found is a new *modus vivendi* in the global environment.

Of course there are mergers or cooperation agreements to achieve the technological, financial and economic size required by the competitive conditions on the world market. True, size is indispensable to create a financial basis for the extensive capital investments and research and development expenditures required for worldwide activities.

But size alone is not sufficient. To penetrate and secure the world market, a long-term strategy is required whose core element is a combination of increased export efforts with simultaneous integration of the exporting companies into the economies of the consuming countries.

This necessitates a broad range of activities that include not only the necessary sales, installation and service organizations—but also direct investments, including manufacturing. Right now, some 50 percent of Siemens' international business is the result of direct investment. This percentage can only increase.

In the United States, for example, Siemens currently operates 52 manufacturing facilities, a major part of the company's $1.7 billion investment there. Products include medical diagnostic imaging equipment, telecommunications systems, factory and automation systems, and semiconductors.

Siemens employs about 25,000 Americans, and the U.S. sales should exceed $3.0 billion for the '87-'88 fiscal year. This produces a very healthy employee-to-sales ratio compared to, say, the ratios of some Japanese companies operating abroad. In addition, 15 percent of Siemens' U.S. sales volume is generated by exports to foreign markets, including Germany. Nearly 80 percent of U.S. revenues represents domestic manufacturing content and other value added elements.

But equally important is our commitment to a healthy American economy. We can make a significant contribution by offering customers productivity enhancement solutions through the products and systems marketed by our various companies.

Successfully meeting the global challenge also involves being able to adapt to new organizational considerations. International business started out with the classic structure common to many companies. There was a headquarters in the home market, and there were subsidiaries abroad. It was a matter of dependence and independence, that is, a strictly vertical relationship.

In the global environment, however, this relationship does not work anymore. One cannot compete in international business over the long term on a dependent/independent basis. An organization can function effectively on an international scale only if there is interdependence—a horizontal relationship possessing many elements of partnership and dialogue. Decisions cannot be dictated. They must be reached, rather, in the spirit and reality of cooperation.

The question is how to achieve this equilibrium. Of course, it can be done by fiat. However, that method never works in the long run. We have to find incentives for people to want to work together and to have an interest in doing so.

In this connection, it is becoming more and more important to supplement local production with local research and development capacities. This puts the company in a position to profit directly from the lead in research and development that a host country may enjoy in a specific field. It also improves the company's own competitive position.

Therefore, an important prerequisite for successful participation in the world market is the timely establishment of future-oriented, local organizations that are able to produce the necessary hardware and software. Long-term thinking and a consistent plan of action are important elements here.

TENACITY, FLEXIBILITY— AND PEOPLE

It has always been a principle of Siemens business strategy abroad not to look for quick profits, but to maintain its commitment even under unfavorable political and economic circumstances. This policy has paid off, despite the criticism leveled at the policy time and time again.

Siemens has a highly diversified range of products that it offers the world market. Its successes are not based on a few products or groups of products with which it floods markets. Instead, it is based on a wide spectrum of goods, usually tailored to specific customer requirements.

One possible way of pursuing the independent approach is via product and system service. Service is a function in defined business sectors that need not be headquartered in the "home market" of the company. It can become a small center of gravity that pulls away from the larger mass of the company headquarters.

This decentralization effect can also be produced by transplanting a product or group of products from the home market to an offshore market. This serves to make entrepreneurs out of the new organization as it works to focus directly on local market needs and expectations.

Then, if the business of a given group, headquartered in the home market, has, for example, 40 percent or more of its business in another market, then people who have product and development responsibility in the home market listen when that new organization, with its 40 percent contribution, speaks.

In addition, you can put the research and development facility—and responsibility—for a given field in a certain country and have this group either work on the development of new products or on the adaptation of the existing products for the local market and standards.

Obviously, this also implies that if one party does not play by the rules of the game, they will get hurt in the process. This is because they are dependent on another party in another context.

It is still true that Siemens is headquartered in West Germany, and that Siemens AG is the shareholder for its other entities doing business around the globe. But what we try to do is differentiate between Siemens AG as a shareholder, and Siemens AG as a partner in supplying products, services, systems, technology and know-how.

When it comes to the role of shareholder, we go, of course, by the normal rule of law that is applicable. When it comes to our other role, we work together in a partnership environment that is accommodating global needs.

What all this leads to is that there are, of course, no ready-made recipes applicable to all international business. We still have to go by the old virtue of having the right product at the right time. We must combine high quality with competitive pricing for the performance and features delivered.

But above all, we need people who understand the business of interdependence, who are willing to accept working as partners in a global activity—and not in a context of dependency or being independent. This, in turn, demands a corporate culture accustomed to thinking on an international scale, a way of thinking responsively to market realities, not the definition of corporate self in myopic, self-determined terms.

You can have everything going for you—product, technology, capital. Yet, it is the human elements, the commitment of people attuned to a transnational, market-driven corporate philosophy, that remains the most important element in the global game—the factor that will increasingly separate the winners from the losers.

James E. Olson

James E. Olson, late chairman and chief executive officer of AT&T, worked in the telephone and telecommunications business since 1943, when he was hired as a splicer's helper with the Northwestern Bell Telephone Company in Grand Forks, North Dakota.

Twenty-three years later, Mr. Olson moved through the ranks of the company to become vice president and general manager in the Iowa area. He was transferred to Indiana Bell as vice president of operations in 1970 and became president of that company two years later.

In 1974, Mr. Olson assumed the presidency of Illinois Bell and, in 1977, became executive vice president of AT&T headquarters in New York City. He was made president and chief operating officer in June 1985, after serving as vice chairman of the board since 1979. He was elected chairman and chief executive officer in 1986. Mr. Olson died April 18, 1988.

Mr. Olson was a graduate of the University of North Dakota.

A director of Warner-Lambert Company, Chase Manhattan, Caterpillar, Inc., Mobil Corporation and other companies and organizations, Mr. Olson also served as trustee of the American Enterprise Institute, The Conference Board and the California Institute of Technology. He was chairman of the U.S.-Japan Council, a member of the Business Roundtable, the Business Council, and the Business Higher Education Forum of the American Council on Education.

4
TOWARD A GLOBAL INFORMATION AGE

James E. Olson
Late Chairman
AT&T, USA

When I assumed duties as Chairman of AT&T in September of 1986, the restructuring of the telecommunications system in the United States was largely complete. The industry had not only been reshaped by the break up of the Bell System, but, just as important, it had been redefined by technological advances and the changing demands and requirements of the marketplace.

The telecommunications systems in the U.S. and around the world were stable and predictable for over a century. But today predictability and stability are gone. Now telecommunications systems around the globe are either currently experiencing fundamental changes, or they've already been reconfigured to fit a competitive model. Government-owned or controlled monopolies that have traditionally governed telecommunications systems almost everywhere in the world are being challenged.

At the heart of this change is the rapid development of advanced information systems and the convergence of two powerful technologies—computers and telecommunications. The most advanced networks today are vast interconnected computer systems, driven by computers and sophisticated software, networks that carry information in all forms over super-fast, high-capacity digital pathways.

Information has become a vital resource for businesses large and small, domestic or foreign. For the largest enterprises, information has been elevated to the status of business asset, as important as raw materials, plant, and employees. Increasingly information is being viewed as a *strategic* asset, not only for business and industry, but for governments as well. Moving and managing it effectively and efficiently is giving companies and nations a competitive advantage in both domestic and global markets.

Today merely moving voices around the nation and the world is not enough to satisfy the growing demands of customers for innovative information services. Other forms of information—data, graphics, and full motion video images— must also be managed and moved swiftly and accurately, and in large volumes.

In this chapter, I will examine the reasons behind the evolution of what is fast becoming a "global information market" as well as where it stands today and where it is heading tomorrow.

THE GLOBALIZATION OF CULTURE

The marketplace for most products and services today is no longer confined to national borders. it has become an international marketplace. The signs are all around us.

Benetton sweaters and Levi's jeans are as common on the streets of London and Tokyo as they are in New York and Rome. Ford Escorts, Hondas, and Mercedes Benz are as common on the highways of Europe and the Far East as they are in North America. There are few major cities in the world where American tourists could not find the familiar golden arches to satisfy a Big Mac attack.

While Americans can view British theatrical productions on public television, audiences in Europe can watch popular American television shows. Versions of "Dallas," for example, are televised in English, French, Flemish, German, and Dutch; an American manager in Brussels refers to Friday night television in Europe as "wall-to-wall 'Dallas.'"

International demand for world-class products is large and growing. Demand worldwide for products made by Gucci, Hitachi, Ford, and even J.R. Ewing make it clear that consumer tastes and preferences are becoming more and more homogeneous and, as a result, a world economy is taking shape.

The evolution of a worldwide marketplace has been stimulated by the need for industries to expand and by mass communications media, which have helped create demand for quality products, no matter who makes them or where they are made. Modern technology has made this new world possible.

THE RISE OF INFORMATION TECHNOLOGY

For most of human history, the relevant marketplace was within walking distance from home. The speed of communication over any sort of distance was directly related to the speed of available transportation. Transportation technology progressed at a painfully slow pace. As Isaac Asimov has pointed out, it took five months for Queen Isabella to learn of Columbus' voyage; two weeks for Europe to learn of President Lincoln's assassination, and 1.3 seconds for the world to witness Neil Armstrong's first step on the moon.

Communication technology left transportation in the dust, so to speak, one day in 1837 when Samuel F. B. Morse transmitted the first electronic impulse on a crude wire line strung between Baltimore and Washington. Four decades later, Alexander Graham Bell sent the first voice message over a wire and the telephone was born. By 1927, when Charles Lindbergh made his historic flight across the Atlantic, AT&T had established the first two-way commercial radio-telephone service between New York and London. A three-minute call cost a staggering $75 (or $482 in 1988 dollars). A three minute call to London today can be made for as little as $2.19.

Less than three decades later, with the completion of the first undersea cable (TAT-1), 36 simultaneous conversations could be carried between America and Europe. On the first day of service, 588 calls were completed over that cable. By comparison, TAT-8, a new transatlantic cable made of optical fibers, will carry up to *40,000* simultaneous calls when it goes into service this year.

The catalyst for the technology explosion we've seen in recent decades can be traced back to the invention of the transistor at AT&T's Bell Laboratories in 1947. That single invention brought about a revolution in computers and other technologies that continues today. Since the 1970s, when the computer industry began its burst of innovation, the ability to store and manipulate information has grown exponentially. Where once it took computers the size of a room to perform a few hundred mathematical operations a second, today's supercomputers can perform billions of operations a second and they take up no more space than a watercooler. In fact, a modern microcomputer chip the size of a fingernail has the same power as the giant computers of 20 years ago.

Advances in silicon technology, electronic transmission, and software systems continue to drive down the costs of processing, storing, managing, and transporting information, while their speed, reliability, and capabilities grow.

No technology has advanced faster than microelectronics—the ability to put hundreds of thousands of transistors and other electronic components on a tiny chip of silicon. Just 15 years ago the 64-bit random access memory (RAM) was introduced. Four years later we had a 4,000-bit RAM. By the beginning of this decade we had a 64,000-bit RAM. Now AT&T is one of several companies that manufacture a 1 million-bit chip with 2 million components per square centimeter. It can store the equivalent of 100 pages of printed text. Only 10 years ago chips were limited to 100 words worth of storage space.

The pace of advance in microelectronics continues to double our capabilities every 18 months. At the current rate of progress, we may achieve 100 million components on a single chip by the turn of the century—which would cut present costs a hundredfold. By the year 2020, it is projected that for $4,000 worth of random access memory, we will be able to store an entire 500,000 volume library. That's less than a penny a book. (If the pace of progress in the auto industry had been similar to that of microelectronics, cars would cost $2.50 and could run 250 miles on a thimble full of gasoline.)

Advances in processing information are being matched by progress in transmitting vast amounts of information. The most spectacular developments have come from the new technology of photonics, in the form of lightwave communications, in which flashes of light from tiny lasers carry voice, video, data—any form of information—through ultrapure glass fibers the diameter of a human hair.

Lightwave systems have higher capacity, are more immune to electrical interference, take much less space underground, and are less expensive to operate than electrical systems that use copper wire. Moreover, photonics is just in its infancy and the promise for the future is only just unfolding. Today, a 30-volume set of the *Encyclopaedia Britannica* can be sent over 40 miles of glass fiber without amplification in a fraction of a second. Lightwave systems are also driving down transmission costs. In 1949, for example, the average investment in a circuit to carry a voice message one mile was $60—in 1949 dollars. Today it costs $10. The new lightwave systems will reduce the investment required to less than a dollar—in the current value of the dollar.

These dramatic cost reductions will also help improve the cost/performance of international communications. The first transatlantic cable had an annual cost per circuit of $250,000. A more recent copper transatlantic cable, put into service in 1976, cost $16,000 per circuit. Our first lightwave cable will drive the cost down to $2,500 per circuit—a reduction factor of 50 in 30 years before discounting for inflation.

A new lightguide system being installed by AT&T between Philadelphia and Chicago will carry the equivalent of more than 24,000 simultaneous 64 kilobit voice conversations on a single pair of glass fibers. That system went into service in mid-1987. AT&T Bell Laboratories scientists have demonstrated the feasibility of boosting capacity to 300,000 voice conversations for each pair of fibers. And even that figure represents but 1 percent of the potential capacity of lightguide fiber.

Software development is also progressing swiftly, though far from the pace of the technologies cited above. But the power and complexity of software controlled communications systems continues to grow, spawning new applications daily.

Once the software bottleneck is opened—and it will be at least widened, if not broken—information movement and management technologies will experience another burst of innovation.

Today's long distance networks are controlled by computerized switchers that depend on software programs. These computers and programs are used to operate AT&T's nationwide network more efficiently. Moreover, they provide the capabilities for introducing new services that require accessing data bases, such as teleconferencing, validating credit cards, or polling.

The complex field of artificial intelligence and robotics is also advancing rapidly. Arthur D. Little estimates that the market for artificial intelligence will grow from about $100 million today to as much as $11 billion by 1990. The industrial robotics market—sized at $200 million today—could grow to $1.5 billion by 1990 and $40 billion by the end of the century.

The deployment of information technology is drawing a new map of the globe. As communications consultant Wilson Dizard, Jr., wrote in his book, *The Coming Age of Information* (Longman, Inc., New York, 1985), the new map is an information grid, comparable to a weather map in that it indicates environmental conditions rather than linear directions. Wrote Dizard: "The map shows a dense mass of organized information over North America, with smaller masses over Europe, Japan, and the Soviet Union. Elsewhere the density of information shades off into thinness. The new technologies can change this map radically by helping create a global knowledge grid."

THE INFORMATION REVOLUTION

Technological advances have played a vital role in bringing about change in the communications industry throughout the world. But technology has not been the only factor in producing fundamental change. Growing competition, shifts in public policy, and the hand of governments have combined to revamp the industry structure.

The same forces that acted to change the U.S. telecommunications industry have combined to produce a similar environment in the international communications market, which is large and rapidly expanding.

The U.S. Department of Commerce's National Telecommunications Information Administration (NTIA) predicts that the global information management and movement market will grow from nearly $500 billion worldwide today, to more than $880 billion by 1990. NTIA estimated the U.S. domestic portion of that market, which includes telecommunications equipment and services as well as computers and computer services, to be $224 billion in 1985. It is expected to grow to nearly $400 billion in the next five years. Clearly the market for moving and managing information is large and fast-growing. While demand levels will vary from country to country, depending on economic conditions and industrial development, people the world over want increased capacity to communicate and to use information.

The growth in telecommunications and data processing markets worldwide is a direct result of the globalization of industries across the board: textiles, machinery, food, finance, petroleum products, metals, education, entertainment, and so on. Production systems of these industries are spread around the globe. To work efficiently, the components of these systems must be tied together with rapid communications, access to common data bases and the use of common information systems.

Very few major businesses today can be purely domestic and hope to thrive for very long. Competition from beyond U.S. borders is heavy and growing daily. More than 70 percent of all American-made products have intense foreign competition in the U.S.

Authors of *The High Flex Society: Shaping America's Economic Future*, Pat Choate and J. K. Linger predict that by the end of this decade, virtually all of America's most productive and advanced industries will face stiff competition. They add that the competitive battle lines will be drawn around the high technology industries such as telecommunications and computers. That's not surprising. After all, with their potential to improve productivity, quality and effectiveness, these industries are crucial to U.S. competitiveness.

Geza Feketekuty, counselor to the U.S. trade representative, has noted the fundamental changes that modern communications systems have produced. Said Feketekuty:

> In the old days, services had to be produced where they were consumed. In the new world, most of the information-based services can be produced anywhere in the world. As long as there is a telephone line. This has led to a new international division of labor, based on a traditional principle of comparative advantage and comparative costs. Engineers in India draw up blueprints that are reviewed by construction company managers in San Francisco and used by construction crews in Saudi Arabia. A credit card transaction in Spain is key punched in Jamaica, processed by computers in London and Arizona and the bill is sent to the card holder in another part of the world. A data processing center in Cleveland serves clients from New York to California during daylight hours, clients from Japan in the early evening hours, then clients in Singapore, followed by Saudi Arabia and Europe in the early morning hours.

In a very real sense, the "Information Age" has already arrived for many businesses. Electronic reservation systems have revolutionized travel. Direct mail catalogs and cable television systems, combined with 800 telephone numbers and computerized order processing systems, are transforming retail merchandizing. Home shopping television programs are already becoming very popular among consumers with cable television.

The financial industry is perhaps the best illustration of the power of information technology, applied to complex problems. Largely because of the power of information technology the size and speed of financial transactions around the world have become truly awesome. The two large U.S. electronic settlements systems—Fedwire and Chips—now clear an average of $1.1 trillion in transactions every business day—six times the daily volume of ten years ago. Worldwide currency trading is now a global around-the-clock business with a daily volume approaching $200 billion. In addition the financial industry has used information technology to produce thousands of new investment instruments and trading strategies, some so complex that only a handful of specialists can really understand them. Some of the world's largest banks are using advanced telecommunications technology for interbank transfers and to connect their offices worldwide. The London-based Barclay's Bank is involved in trading more than $9 billion each day with a staff of 140 people. Technology has made it possible for so few to do so much.

The New York Times highlighted the pace of change in the world currency markets in an article published in March of 1987. The Times pointed out that it was only 20 years ago that telexes replaced cablegrams for the handling of transatlantic transactions, turning into a few minutes what once took several hours. By 1970 the telephone replaced telex as the preferred medium of exchange. Then, just four years ago, the Reuters Network, combined with computers and video screens, launched the global currency market into instant access and instant transactions.

Information has almost become as valuable as money itself to the worldwide financial community.

Modern information technology is also providing a competitive edge for retailers. The Italian-based Benetton Group made an impressive drive into the U.S. fashion market with the help of computers and communications. By wiring their retail knitwear stores to computers and linking this network to its headquarters in northern Italy, Benetton gathered almost instant information on styles and colors that were selling. Acting on this information, orders could be sent to factories with directions for dying wool in the proper colors and retail outlets would be stocked within days with the most marketable products. London's famed Harrod's Department Store has marketed its products directly to American consumers during peak buying seasons, using International 800 Service, which permits customers in the U.S. to use toll-free lines to place their orders.

The automobile industry is using sophisticated information systems to compete in world markets. Toyota, for example, plans to deploy an international value-added network that will connect it to thousands of suppliers. Ford is linking its global operation in pursuit of world cars. Mazda is building a private telecommunications system to connect its Hiroshima headquarters with subsidiaries around the world. General Motors is using information technology on a massive scale to give it the capability of designing a product in Germany, manufacturing it in Korea, and then processing the data into an assembly line located in the United States. GM is also developing sophisticated automation systems for its factories that will give it yet another competitive advantage in world markets.

These are only a few examples of what companies across industry are doing with state-of-the-art communications systems. It is obvious to these firms and others that efficient movement and management of information is no longer a business convenience, but a business necessity. Information has become a key to productivity improvement at home and a requirement for world-class products abroad.

THE ECONOMICS OF INFORMATION

Advances in information technologies have had a more powerful impact on the U.S. economy than even the optimists once predicted, according to Ambassador Diana Lady Dougan, U.S. coordinator and director of the Bureau of International Communications and Information Policy. Said Ambassador Dougan:

> Advances in computer sciences have not only unshackled man's mind, but unleashed new economic forces which could not have been envisioned even a few years ago. Over the last two decades, the creation, processing and distribution of information has moved from an incidental support function to the center stage of American industry. Of the 19 million new jobs created in the U.S. during the 1970s, close to 90 percent were white-collar jobs. The proportion of the U.S. work force in information-related jobs is now over 60 percent.

Ambassador Dougan also pointed out that telecommunications and information equipment and services now represent the nation's third largest area of export—totaling nearly $40 billion.

However, while the United States has opened its telecommunications market to foreign competition, other nations have not reciprocated. As a result, U.S. imports of telecommunications equipment more than tripled between 1982 and 1985 and are now running well above $2 billion a year, while exports are running at an annual rate of less than $1 billion. The trade deficit in telecommunications equipment in 1986 was $1.9 billion. Just four years earlier, the U.S. had a *surplus* of $275 million.

The world economy is operating under trade policies established more than 40 years ago and which were aimed at rebuilding industrial economies ravaged by World War II. These policies helped sustain the rapid growth in world trade to its current level of two trillion dollars a year. However, conditions have changed substantially and trade policies have not followed suit. Telecommunications issues have become so vital to the nation that they have been pushed to the top of the agenda in bilateral trade discussions between the U.S. and a number of countries, including Japan and Germany. For example, the General Agreement on Tariffs and Trade (GATT) does not cover services—a crucial area of concern in the telecommunications and information equipment industries that was not a factor four decades ago. There is growing support among leaders of American industry to press GATT negotiators to include services in the trade mix.

There will be political barriers to overcome of course. Service trade involves the flow of information across borders, a flow that many governments want to limit for reasons of national security, political ideology, or even cultural autonomy.

Those who continue to resist free trade and who try to block the flow of information into their nations are fighting a losing battle. Eventually, technology, not politics, will determine the availablity of information to the world population. Individuals and nations who recognize and act progressively will find themselves a quantum leap ahead of those who insist on living with the policies and practices of the past.

The information movement and management industry represents a critical infrastructure for the national economy. To the extent that the industry is innovative, responsive, and efficient, it invigorates the economy. It lowers costs and enhances productivity throughout business and industry. If, on the other hand, the pace of innovation in the information industry is sluggish, response to market needs slows, opportunities to boost productivity and lower costs decrease, and the entire economy suffers.

In short, since the information industry is one upon which all others draw in the production and distribution of goods and services, it can limit or liberate a nation's economy. This becomes especially important when considering America's declining stature in the world marketplace and its $170 billion trade deficit.

America has not come close to reaping the full benefits of the information technology it has available. Part of the problem is the change in technology itself—especially in computer and communications technologies. These technologies can no longer be viewed as fully separate. The line that once distinguished computing from communicating has all but been obliterated.

And yet computers and communications continue to exist largely as separate systems. Where advanced information technologies are in place, many exist as stand-alone systems, creating isolated islands of information across the country. They have not been interconnected and thus their full benefits, including substantial cost savings and efficient new applications, have not been realized.

The missing links between information processing and communications systems present a major challenge to industry, particularly the information movement and management industry. That is a challenge AT&T is addressing in a major way by integrating information technologies and bringing more of their benefits to the public. AT&T is using its technology and its strong skills in communications networking to lash together those islands of information and enable customers to manage and move their information in ways that solve problems rather than create them.

Technological incompatibility is not just a U.S. problem. It's also a major problem within and between nations the world over, a widely recognized issue that is being seriously addressed by industry policymakers. The International Telecommunications Union (ITU) is one of the key organizations addressing the question of compatibility of networks and information equipment. Considerable progress has already been made in system design as well as in setting international standards. The U.S. and the European Economic Council are holding regular discussions aimed at achieving compatibility between networks in the first formal attempt to establish a joint approach in telecommunications.

One of the most promising signs of progress is the development of the Integrated Services Digital Network (ISDN) standard. Communications firms around the world are working together under this common standard to ensure that one day people everywhere will be able to send or access information in any form from any point on Earth as easily as they can communicate with a neighbor.

AN INFORMATION AGE STRATEGY

AT&T's strategy for the Information Age is not confined to the shores of North America. And AT&T is not venturing into global markets with its eyes closed. AT&T has considerable experience in global markets. It has been linking countries and continents by cable and satellites for the past seven decades. Today AT&T provides connections to more than 250 countries and territories around the globe.

AT&T's role as an international carrier has had to expand to keep pace with a rapidly growing demand for international communications. International calling is growing at a rate of 25 percent a year. In 1965 AT&T transmitted 3 million international telephone calls. In 1985 that figure was 707 million.

In addition to regular long-distance voice communications service, in the last three years AT&T has extended the types of custom communications services provided domestically to virtually all international points customers need to reach.

The international communications service business has spurred the development of international trade, finance and information exchange. By expanding links between nations, a worldwide infrastructure has evolved, an infrastructure that will be the foundation of a global information age.

Of course, global communications pathways are just a part of the building blocks for the information age. Computerized communications equipment and software systems—or applications—are equally important in forging the Information Age.

AT&T is addressing the global market for information movement and management with a strategy that targets its resources on the key markets of Western Europe, the Far East, and North America. AT&T is strengthening its networking capabilities—for data as well as voice—and is concentrating on delivering innovative applications for sale to large multinational firms and to governments around the world.

AT&T has restructured its operations to reflect its international focus by assigning top-level managers in each business unit to market products throughout the world. Thus international concerns have become a basic consideration in product and market planning throughout the business. At the same time, a staff of managers, located abroad, are responsible for all AT&T operations within specific countries. This is a major departure from the past, when the international market was addressed by AT&T managers based in the United States.

AT&T currently has sales offices in Australia, Belgium, Brazil, Canada, the People's Republic of China, Egypt, France, the Federal Republic of Germany, Hong Kong, Ireland, Italy, Japan, Korea, Mexico, Puerto Rico, Saudi Arabia, Singapore, Spain, Taiwan, Thailand, and the United Kingdom. AT&T products are sold in 90 countries.

Being there, however, does not necessarily mean one has a market presence. In a very real sense, AT&T is a newcomer to the global marketplace for information movement and management equipment. That means AT&T must build a reputation throughout the world. AT&T is not a household name in Europe and Japan as it is in the U.S. In most of the world, AT&T is recognizable only to a few—such as the managers of the PTTs (government-owned foreign telephone companies), or members of the scientific community who know that Bell Laboratories is part of AT&T.

Since few customers in any area of the world are trusting enough to buy a million-dollar piece of equipment from an unknown firm, AT&T has had to look for effective ways to build its reputation and, at the same time, get started in markets that are difficult to enter.

Telecommunications remains one of the most protected sectors in world trade. No other industry is so inhibited by national regulation. Stiff trade barriers remain in some of the biggest world markets, while the U.S. market is open to all comers.

The trade restrictions vary from country to country and some are more obvious than others. For example, some countries have restrictions on international electronic data transmission while others set market quotas on foreign equipment sales and even prohibit such sales. In some cases, technical standards for equipment are established to favor domestic firms over outsiders. In other countries, taxes and tariffs discriminate against imports. These are just a few of the barriers to market entry U.S. firms face when they seek to market their products overseas.

To gain entry to such markets, AT&T has elected to form strategic alliances with major foreign firms. One such alliance involves AT&T and Olivetti. AT&T owns a 25 percent share in the Italian firm that supplies the AT&T 6300 personal computer and markets AT&T's line of 3Bs. Olivetti is also marketing AT&T's digital switchboards in the European market.

Other AT&T joint ventures and partnerships with foreign firms include:

- APT, a venture with N. V. Philips of the Netherlands, to sell switching and transmission equipment in Europe.
- AT&T, British Telecom and Kokusai Denshin Denwa, Ltd., to provide one-stop shopping for private-line telecommunications service between locations in the U.S., Great Britain, and Japan.
- Nordic Cable and Wire of Denmark, to manufacture optical fiber and market it in Scandinavia and elsewhere in Europe.
- Goldstar Semiconductor, a venture with the Lucky Goldstar Group of the Republic of Korea to manufacture and sell electronic switching equipment, fiber optic cable, and 3B computers in the Far East.
- AT&T Taiwan Telecommunications, Inc., a four-way partnership for manufacturing electronic switchers in Taiwan.

- AT&T Microelectronica de Espana, a venture with Telefonica, the Spanish telephone company, to manufacture custom-made integrated circuits for the European market.

These are a few of the more than 20 joint ventures and partnerships that AT&T has formed to market or manufacture products abroad. Negotiations with other firms will undoubtedly produce more such ventures in the future.

So AT&T is fully cognizant of the opportunities and obstacles it faces in marketing its information equipment, communications systems, and customer applications around the world.

To summarize, AT&T is responding to the global market in three major ways. First, it is strengthening its international communications services operations.

Second, it is marketing switching and transmission equipment to government-owned and private telephone companies throughout the world. Third, it is concentrating its resources on business and government customers who have major requirements for information movement and management systems. Those customers are located primarily in the highly developed and fastest growing countries in Western Europe, the Far East, and North America.

AT&T intends to play a major role in building that new global information map envisioned by author Wilson Dizard. How that map will look by the end of the century depends on how free companies are to innovate and market information products worldwide and to what extent political, economic, and ideological factors come into play to spur or delay progress.

The shape of the future—of the coming Age of Information—depends on the strategies and actions we choose today and in the decade ahead. The strategies and actions of countries, of industries, and of companies collectively will determine how swiftly society moves on to its next promising chapter.

Paul H. O'Neill

Paul H. O'Neill was elected chairman of the board and chief executive officer of Alcoa on April 20, 1987, after serving as director of the company.

Prior to joining Alcoa, Mr. O'Neill was president of the International Paper Company. He had joined International Paper in 1977 as vice president—planning and finance. In 1983, he was again promoted, this time to senior vice president of the company's paperboard and packaging segment. He was named president two years later.

Mr. O'Neill received a B.A. degree in economics from Fresno State College and a master's degree in public administration from Indiana University. He also participated in graduate studies programs in economics at Claremont Graduate School and George Washington University. He began his career as a computer systems analyst with the U.S. Veteran's Administration and later worked as an engineer for Morrison-Knudsen, Inc., in Anchorage, Alaska. He served on the staff of the U.S. Office of Management and Budget from 1967 to 1977 and was deputy director of the OMB from 1974 to 1977.

In addition to his work for Alcoa, Mr. O'Neill is a director of National Westminster Bank and Manpower Research Group.

5
QUALITY AND EFFICIENCY— THE KEYS TO THE GLOBAL MARKET

Paul H. O'Neill
Chairman and Chief Executive Officer
Alcoa Aluminum Company, USA

As 1988 began, America's basic industries found a better economic environment than they had experienced since 1980. The outlook in early 1988 was perhaps fragile, but balances between supply and demand, prices and costs were in better shape than they had been for years.

There is, unfortunately, a great danger in the prospect that managements will extrapolate these conditions, assuming that the recent past misery of basic industry was an aberration. More likely, however, is that the conditions we see today are a cyclical phenomenon that need to be separated from long-term trend conditions in order for us to accurately forecast what the future holds in store. Since the 1950s, we in America have been getting trend signals from the world economy, and to a large extent we have ignored them or rationalized them away. As our relative position in the world economy has been reduced, a variety of explanations has been offered:

Some have argued that other nations were advantaged by the fact that their industrial structure was destroyed in the Second World War and, therefore, as they rebuilt their economies they did so with more modern equipment and technology than existed in U.S. industry.

- Allied to this view is one that says governments have subsidized the creation of unfair foreign competition. Some even credit the U.S. government with subsidizing competition through trade policy or by supporting low-cost development loans to competitors in many countries.
- Others have argued our relative decline is caused by much lower labor rates in other countries.
- Still others have claimed that the international playing field is tilted against us by tariff and non-tariff barriers to our products.
- Bad government policy has been pointed out as a culprit in our competitive position—too much government spending, or taxes, or both; deficits and government debt a major contributor to unfavorable exchange rates; excessive safety and environmental regulations leading to higher costs.
- Some have identified spiraling energy costs as a major contributor to our changed position.

While there is room to argue the validity of these points, individually and collectively, none of them deals with the most profound change in our standing among competing nations. That change has to do with the quality of our products and the efficiency of our operations—two very closely related issues.

QUALITY AND EFFICIENCY

As a general matter, the quality of our products and the efficiency of our operations have continued to improve over the years. We are not worse than we were. The products coming out of American factories today are clearly better than they were 10, or 20, or 30 years ago. For example, the newest model-year automobiles, as compared to those of 30 years ago, are safer, more durable, and more fuel efficient by almost any measure. And, on a constant dollar basis, they are less expensive.

But, better than last year isn't good enough anymore, nor is "better than our domestic competition." Our challenge now is to be better than the rest of the world. This is where all of the rationalizations offered for our diminished position fail to provide comfort, for none helps explain the fact that Americans are buying more foreign products because the quality is better, not because of a lower price.

To understand our changed position in quality, it is useful to compare our position today and 30 years ago to, for example, the position of Korea today and 30 years ago, in the automobile industry. Thirty years ago we had more than 50 years of experience in manufacturing automobiles on a huge scale. We invented factory assembly lines, and we had no effective competition in the world for the mass market. By comparison, Korea in the late 1950s had no tradition of manufacturing and, for practical purposes, no automobile industry. Thirty years later, Korean automobiles took over the leading import position in Canada—18 months after they introduced their product into the market. Obviously, the Koreans didn't follow our path in establishing their position. Effectively, they became a real competitor in a complex product market in one decade. There are several important points in this illustration.

- New competitors can start with the current state of the art in any product because technology and know-how are increasingly portable across national boundaries.
- New competitors are not bound to the current quality/ efficiency standards of existing competitors.
- Capital will flow to promising business opportunities, even if the host country has a war-torn environment with an agrarian tradition.
- Massive scale of operations provides no lasting protection for existing competitors.

There are examples, much like the Korean automobile case, in most important markets today, even in the basic industries.

Aluminum Company of America was presented with its own vivid experience when it acquired aluminum material from a Japanese company to check the competitive quality and found, to everyone's amazement, the Japanese product quality surpassed even the highest expectations of what Alcoa had planned to achieve. Initially, the reaction was a rationalization—the Japanese material had been specially produced; it could not be standard production quality. But the rationalizations didn't hold up. The Japanese product was from their standard production run, even though it was far better than Alcoa's best product.

Similarly, International Paper Company found that the Japanese insistence on tighter specifications for material used to make corrugated boxes was not a "non-tariff" barrier as some of its managers first charged. Linerboard, the outer layers of paper used to produce a corrugated box, has been produced in huge volumes in the United States for decades. Over the years, specifications for the product have evolved, one of the most important being the moisture content, which directly affects the speed of boxmaking. In the early 1980s the U.S. standard was 5 percent moisture—plus or minus 3 percentage points—or a range of 2 percent moisture to 8 percent moisture.

When U.S. producers began to call on Japanese companies to sell them the product, the Japanese said they were interested in being customers, but the specification for moisture content would have to be 5 percent, plus or minus one percentage point; a range of 4 percent to 6 percent. The reaction of U.S. manufacturing executives was to say this standard was unnecessary—after all, the U.S. was making fine boxes with its easier standard—and undoable because the paper manufacturing process could not produce to such fine tolerances.

The Japanese persisted, offering samples of product that already met their specifications—from their own production, from Scandanavian production and from South African production. Further, they demonstrated that material produced to their specifications had a profound effect on the economics of boxmaking. Using material produced to their specifications they were able to produce boxes 38 percent faster than was possible with linerboard produced to the conventional U.S. specification. Faced with these facts, U.S. manufacturing plant people said, yes, they could see the value and they would begin producing to the Japanese specification—but they would need over $100 million of new equipment in order to produce at these tighter tolerance levels.

In fact, today, U.S. producers of linerboard are producing material for the Japanese market to the Japanese standard, *and* they did not spend hundreds of millions of dollars to upgrade their production equipment. What they did instead was to accept the Japanese standard as a legitimate one and begin to work systematically on meeting it by bringing their manufacturing processes under operating control. Rather than getting by with what was "good enough," they began to push toward new definitions of quality performance. As someone has said, they realized that "good enough was not good anymore!" As manufacturing people worked toward the new standard, they found that manufacturing costs *went down* as they brought their process under control because they made much less scrap product.

These illustrations help frame the challenge for the U.S. in the years ahead. Fundamentally the challenge is competition. In a sense, it is a renewal of circumstances that we in the U.S. enjoyed for decades when *we* were the aggressive competitor. We developed our natural resources, educated our population, invented new processes, created larger scale manufacturing plants, developed markets—in effect, controlled and created the rules of economic competition as we went along. We were the driver.

A GLOBAL PERSPECTIVE

We can be the driver again, but to do so we must change in some radical ways. The most dramatic and overarching change required is a change in perspective. Contrary to our successful domestic perspective of the past, we must become global in our analysis and understanding of competition, both current and prospective.

When America defined the global standard, it was sufficient to set our standards by our own past performance characteristics and those of our U.S. competitors. As an example, in those easier days it was acceptable to agree to industry pattern bargaining for wage rates because the practice insured that no individual competitor was advantaged or disadvantaged by labor relations. This meant that competition centered around product innovation, and the ability of each firm to organize and manage its resources. Further, under these conditions of domestically defined competition, the interaction between U.S. companies established world prices.

These circumstances of the past are disappearing, most clearly for large multinational corporations. But, the consequences of real global competition will be felt even in neighborhood businesses in the next century. McDonald's success in taking its quality product concept around the world is a leading indicator of the way business is likely to be conducted in the future. Because of the rapidly developing portability of knowledge and capital, the new perspective of global competition will be important even to those whose only ambition is to serve a local market in one country.

This concept of a global perspective will be important in the future to every aspect of a U.S. firm's ability to compete. Again, in the past, our battles over the roles of federal, state, and local government—and their tax and regulatory policies—have been family squabbles. Whatever the outcomes of these squabbles, the ultimate impact was a U.S. impact and, at least for federal actions, U.S. firms were impacted in roughly equal ways. And, when we led the world, the impact of regulations and taxes could be recovered in the price of the product. With world competition setting prices, this "pass-along" capability has disappeared and, importantly, the general or average cost of government is no longer relevant to an individual firm or industry. What is important is the comparative cost of government to the competing firms or industry across the world economy. This suggests a much more complex problem for U.S. governments. It also suggests an entirely new constraint on Congress, which in the past felt no need to consider the competitive impact of taxation. Most likely, this new dimension in our policy formulation will force a movement to a consumption tax or some equivalent device in the next 10 or 20 years, because there is no other way to neutralize the impact of taxes on international competition.

Additionally, the importance of every cost to our ability to compete will bring heightened attention to the need to eliminate inefficiency in government, simply because we will not be able to survive with inefficiency. The old chestnut of bad utilization of resources (such as keeping World War II military installations going simply because we could afford it) will have to give way to a national determination to maintain our standard of living by relentlessly driving out waste.

If we can make this change in perspective, our prospects for reestablishing our preeminent position in the world will improve dramatically because, in an analytic sense, our recent and growing disadvantage is not mysterious.

LESSONS FROM GLOBAL COMPETITORS

As one looks at the best of foreign competitors there are certain clear threads in their pattern of success. First, our toughest competitors are doing a better job than we in their utilization of human resources. Where we have concentrated on reducing the labor content of our products, they have concentrated on enabling their people to help improve the process, and thereby the product. Where we have concentrated on simplifying our process through even greater mechanization, they have concentrated on doing an even better job of understanding their process and methodically eliminating process variability. Where we have sought to reduce our vulnerability to our work force, they have increased their work force's sense of participation. Where we have left the training of our work force to the "hand-me-down," on-the-job art form, they have dedicated substantial time and resources to giving every employee the training they deed to assess quantitatively and improve the product of their work. Where we have applied the military model of layered and compartmentalized authority, they have emphasized the authority of knowledge and minimal layers of organization. Where we have tended toward the idea of the superstar performer, they have tended toward the importance of every individual as a member of the team.

Their models for utilization of individuals are working better than ours. We need to change ours.

In the process of changing, we need to establish a new template for judging how, and on what, we spend our resources. The essence of this new template is to evaluate every expenditure against the question of whether our customers should be expected to pay for the expenditure in the price of the product or service we provide. For small firms this may seem to be a strange test, because they already face this test every day. But in many large corporations, practices have developed over the past century that will not meet this test. For example, in the era of global competition, corporate dining rooms, chauffeured limousines, and other convenient non-necessities that do not contribute to the value of the product for the customer cannot survive. Expense account excesses and departments without salable products will also disappear.

The second thread to successful foreign competition is their fixation on quality. The best competitors are dedicated to the notion of doing everything correctly the first time a task is done. Their secret to producing high quality goods is not to inspect each product before it is shipped. Rather they strive not to produce defective products. Where our general philosophy is to provide long warranties to fix products that break, their philosophy is to make products that don't break.

The third thread of successful foreign competition is, in a way, a blending of the first two threads—attention to detail. Where we forgive ourselves paying attention to the 80 percent of things that "don't count," they worry about every detail of every activity, every day. There are no unimportant or less important activities in the work of successful foreign competitors. In contrast, we have been through a variety of cycles when marketing was the most important, or finance was the most important, or labor relations was the most important—or, long ago, manufacturing was the most important. In the new era, successful firms will ensure that every activity is important, or it will be eliminated.

A fourth thread of successful foreign competition is a much shorter time cycle than the U.S. experience in applying better ideas to everyday practice. This is an area of great potential for U.S. firms because the observable spread between what we know how to do and what we actually practice is very significant. In this area, we need to break down the barriers between our laboratories and our operations.

EDUCATION AND THE GLOBAL CHALLENGE

There is a related challenge in all of the threads of foreign competition for our formal educational process. We need a much closer relationship between our academic community and our operating firms. Today, few if any universities are schooling their students in the new imperatives of global competition. In order to bridge this gap, it may be necessary to rethink the internal organizational form of our universities. The deficiency in the current organizational form is that its major dimension is individual and independent academic disciplines—the various branches of engineering (civil, mechanical, chemical, electrical) statistics, finance, etc.

The need for the future is to educate our students in these disciplines related to systems and processes, subordinating the independent importance of the disciplines to the interdependent demands of working in the context of systems and process flows that necessitate teamwork. This will be a difficult change because the tradition of academia is the tradition of the individual with jealously guarded boundaries around the reward and recognition process.

ADMONITIONS

In all of these things we need a sense of urgency. Markets once lost to competition will be exceedingly difficult to recover. Further, the process of improvement in the best foreign firms is continuing, methodically, day-by-day. Every day that we are not improving at the same rate, we are losing ground.

Having observed actions that will make a difference in our competitive position, it is worth noting, in conclusion, some actions that will not help.

At the governmental level, trade barriers against better value foreign products are not in our real interest. Shielding U.S. firms from the best foreign competition will only insure that we will become a second-rate nation in the next century. Nor is there any clear, major role for the federal government through the legislative process. This is not to say that government should simply keep out of the way. Far from it. The federal government should take on the role of enabler, helping to assure that all necessary components to a competitive nation are in place. If we are to regain our competitive position, the improvement will have to occur in individual firms and industries, with the initiative flowing from those sources, not from government.

At the level of the firm, financial restructuring, plant closings, and other actions that do not fundamentally change the traditional approach to the business will not produce the needed, lasting effects required by global competition. These actions may be necessary, useful, and supportive of fundamental change, but taken alone, they will only create a temporary illusion of improvement.

Edmund T. Pratt, Jr.

Since 1972 Edmund T. Pratt, Jr., has been chairman and chief executive officer of Pfizer, Inc., one of the nation's most widely deployed multinational companies.

Mr. Pratt began his business career at IBM in the late 1940s. By 1958, he was comptroller of the IBM World Trade Corporation. During the Kennedy administration, Mr. Pratt left IBM to serve as assistant secretary of the Army for financial management. Mr. Pratt left the Pentagon to join Pfizer, first as corporate comptroller and later as head of the company's overseas operations.

A graduate of Duke University with a degree in electrical engineering, Mr. Pratt continued his studies at the University of Pennsylvania, where he earned an MBA degree from the Wharton School of Commerce and Finance.

In addition to his work at Pfizer, Mr. Pratt serves as director of General Motors, International Paper, and Chase Manhattan corporations. He represents the U.S. private sector as a member of the President's Advisory Committee for Trade Negotiations and is a past chairman of the committee. He is chairman of the Emergency Committee for American Trade, a group comprising over 60 of the largest U.S. companies engaged in global commerce, and cochairman of the Business Roundtable and a member of its policy committee. Mr. Pratt is also a member of the Business Council. In recent years, Mr. Pratt has also served as chairman of Governor Cuomo's Advisory Board, the New York Chamber of Commerce and Industry, and New York City Partnership.

6
GROWING TO SERVE THE GLOBAL MARKETPLACE

Edmund T. Pratt, Jr.
Chairman and Chief Executive Officer
Pfizer Inc., USA

Every morning thousands of people pass below my Manhattan office window on their way to work. Nearby, hundreds of thousands more scatter from Grand Central Station, to nearby buildings. Indeed, all over Manhattan, morning commuters stream from train stations and subway tunnels to towers of granite and glass.

Why is this remarkable? To begin with, these are free people—and that is rarity enough in the history of this planet. More than any general population in history, they lead lives of their own making and choosing.

To be sure, they have personal obligations and responsibilities. Occasionally, this person will dream of a tropical isle and that person of uninterrupted decades of play on uncrowded golf courses, but few of them fly off to these dreamlands. On the whole, they do not really consider work as Adam's curse. Instead, these people—and hundreds of millions of people like them in America and elsewhere on the globe—espouse another view of work. They know that there is more to be said for it than merely that "it pays the bills"— though that in itself is no small matter.

As participants in the modern world's preeminent economic

organization, the corporation, they have learned from experience that there are few hurdles that cannot be cleared by people working to meet common ends. They like that idea. They like doing things, and getting things done. And it's a good thing they do—because, for employees of high-technology, highly-regulated companies such as Pfizer, each day brings plenty of hurdles to leap.

And there's something else. When honest with themselves, especially in the quieter moments of life, most consider work among their truest blessings. For work transforms a necessity (the need all of us have to feed and house ourselves and our families), into an opportunity to contribute something to our world and our children's. In so doing, our work helps invest our lives with meaning, and contributes to the greatest treasure we can ever possess, a sense of our own usefulness.

Some critics might complain that this view is far from universal; they're right. They would argue that for most people in the world work is still drudgery, a quest not for satisfaction but for daily bread.

Yet scores of millions more people consider work as something beyond mere drudgery today than they did only a decade or two ago—not even to mention any earlier time. Each year, not merely in the United States, or Europe, or Japan, but wherever economic freedom has allowed men and women the opportunity to improve their condition, and in so doing supply products and services to their fellow citizens, more and more people embrace this alternative view of work. Why? Because they have experience of it as being true.

I would not be surprised if, along with the general extension of liberty, this new and nobler view of work were to be America's lasting legacy to the world. If so, it will have been carried to the earth's far corners by people such as the men and women I see each morning. In other words, the kind of people who work for Pfizer in more than 100 countries throughout the world, and for thousands of other companies in the United States and abroad.

This changing view of work and, more generally, of the capabilities of free men and women working together toward a common purpose, has been wrought—more than by any other single force—by employees of the least understood, most needlessly maligned institution in the world today, the multinational corporation.

I am a businessman, the head of a large and complex organization. That gives me plenty to do, and I learned long ago that no one can do everything. Thus like most people in business, for the most part I leave the theoretical discussions of multinational corporations to others—academic economists, college professors, clerics, and politicians. Unfortunately, relative to the general population, few of these discussants have ever worked for a multinational corporation; many have never worked for a profit-making organization of any kind.

As a result, there is a chasm of considerable breadth between the people who work for multinational companies and those who talk and write about them. This gap is reflected in the fact that most such discussions are marred by a paucity of first-hand experience and a dearth of specificity.

It is my hope that this article will help partially to bridge the chasm. Perhaps by explaining in some detail the development, accomplishments, and everyday frustrations of one multinational corporation—a high-technology enterprise coping with strict, varying, and sometimes discriminatory regulations everywhere it operates—some misconceptions about "The Multinational Corporation" can be laid to rest. In any case, I think it's worth the trouble to try.

A BRIEF HISTORY

Like every great commercial enterprise, Pfizer Inc. began as the earnest ambition of unknown men. Charles Pfizer and his cousin, Charles Erhart, were natives of Germany. Full of the ideas of liberty then stirring Europe, they sought new lives in the land that had already attained the political and economic freedom for which they longed. Though young men (Pfizer was 25; Erhart, 28), shortly after their arrival in the United States, they opened a business in Brooklyn, New York, in 1849. Their goal was to manufacture "fine chemicals"—small quantities of chemicals of the highest quality.

A year later, with the help of a loan of $2,500 from Pfizer's father, they bought a brick building on Bartlett Street. That original Pfizer building is still in use today.

The upstart company's first product was santonin, commonly called Levant wormseed. By 1855, they had begun manufacturing various iodine preparations as well, and shortly thereafter introduced a line of mercurials. By the start of America's Civil War, they had added borax, boric acid, and refined camphor to their list of products. Many of these product lines remained profitable well into the 20th century.

Two additional products were extremely important to the company in its first half-century and more. First, in the early 1860s, utilizing their connections in Europe, the founders made arrangements to import the basic ingredient required to manufacture cream of tartar and tartaric acid. The products, manufactured at the works in Brooklyn, were sold widely to bakers and beverage manufacturers, and for domestic use. Then, beginning in 1880, Pfizer began the manufacture of citric acid, which had numerous medicinal and culinary uses. By the end of the 19th century, the firm was selling its products throughout the United States, and even had begun exporting small quantities of chemicals to Mexico, South America, the West Indies, Europe, India, and Australia.

In 1891, Charles Erhart passed away, and in the years that followed, Charles Pfizer began to prepare for his own retirement. In 1900, the company was incorporated. By 1905, day-to-day operations had officially passed outside the family, to an energetic long-time employee, John Anderson.

Yet for generations the company maintained the aura of a family-owned business. This sense of working for "the world's largest family business" is at the very core of Pfizer's operating principles—of our corporate culture.

In the last century, it often happened that several generations of the same family worked for Pfizer. Tenures were measured in decades—three, four, even six in the case of one of my earliest predecessors as chief executive officer. Long tenures and family-company loyalty remain a hallmark of Pfizer today.

The company continued much in this way, growing steadily and conservatively, until the Second World War. Then a remarkable discovery called penicillin, and the desperate need for massive quantities of it at the battle fronts, catapulted the company into a new period in its history.

Penicillin, though discovered, had never been produced in significant quantities by the time the U.S. entered the war. It was an extremely unstable material with a short shelf life. Many companies struggled with the problem of how to mass produce penicillin. It was Pfizer, however, which pioneered the most successful method, deep-tank fermentation. By 1944, Pfizer was making more than half the penicillin manufactured by the 21 companies involved in U.S. wartime production, and consistently exceeding government production targets.

Following the war's end, penicillin was made available for civilian use; Pfizer made 85 percent of the penicillin sold. Because Pfizer itself was not in the pharmaceutical marketing business, however, the drug was retailed under other companies' labels. It was not long, however, before the pharmaceuticals companies built their own plants to manufacture penicillin. Pfizer's heroic wartime efforts now counted for little.

Pfizer's penicillin orders plummeted. As a result of this experience, when Pfizer discovered another wonder drug, Terramycin (oxytetracycline), late in the decade, it decided to market this and future Pfizer discoveries under the Pfizer name.

Terramycin was produced by a new soil organism. Itself nontoxic, it proved powerfully effective in combatting such bacterial killers as streptococci, staphlococci, and pneumococci. In all, it was found to be effective in the treatment of more than a hundred diseases, and to have numerous non-medical uses.

In March 1950, Terramycin received federal Food and Drug Administration (FDA) approval. Within two years, sales of the drug went from a standing start to some $45 million. Our Groton (Connecticut) works—opened because the Brooklyn works could be expanded no further—quickly became the largest fermentation plant in the world, with more than 50 buildings in use.

After a century of specializing in fine chemicals, penicillin and Terramycin had made Pfizer a pharmaceuticals company. By the 1950s, spurred by worldwide demand for Terramycin, the company was also on its way to becoming a modern multinational corporation.

After a century without significant overseas business, Pfizer began seriously marketing abroad in the years following the Second World War. It opened an office at its Maiden Lane headquarters in Manhattan to develop non-U.S. accounts in 1947. The operation had five employees.

The early strategy was to appoint agents in nations throughout South America, and to build upon the prewar business contacts the company had in Europe. Furthermore, the decision was made to sell products abroad under Pfizer's own label (something the company at that time had never yet done in the U.S.). By the late 1940s, Pfizer's export business had grown from virtually nothing to $9 million.

Beginning in Canada, Mexico, Cuba, England, and Belgium, Pfizer established subsidiaries in each country in which it sought to do business. Thus, in the early 1950s, spurred by sales of Terramycin and a new approach to non-U.S. business, the company's international receipts skyrocketed.

Operating on the principle that the way to "go international" was to "go local," my predecessors realized that subsidiary companies were better equipped than any central office to handle sales in their particular areas. With their intimate knowledge of their country and its regulatory restrictions, local personnel could best cope with specific markets, currency exchange problems, and the myriad other difficulties involved in the importation of pharmaceuticals.

In fact, this strategy made a virtue of necessity. For it was the *only* way that Pfizer (and many other companies, in our industry and others) *could* operate abroad. As a practical matter, though the need for antibiotics and other drugs overseas was enormous, the weakness of national currencies after the war made hopes of large-scale trade unrealistic. Furthermore, we were legally proscribed in many countries from importing finished dosage forms or even bulk drugs. Consequently, in order to do business, we were forced to construct manufacturing facilities (for example, in England, Spain, Portugal, Greece, and Turkey, to cite just a portion of the European examples alone).

In the next two decades, staggering effort went into building

Pfizer's international operations. The number of our subsidiaries grew by leaps. We began manufacturing abroad. We bought some highly respected companies in Europe, and established our presence around the globe. By the mid-1960s, Pfizer's strategy of decentralization—leaving local decision making in the hands of the local managers on the scene—had made Pfizer one of history's most successful multinational corporations.

Today Pfizer is a $5 billion company, one of the largest pharmaceutical companies in the world. Over 60 percent of sales and the bulk of our operating profit come from the health-care segment of our business, which includes pharmaceuticals and medical devices. Other businesses include specialty chemicals, agricultural products, cosmetics, over-the-counter health products, and specialty pigments, metals and minerals. Roughly 50 percent of our sales are outside the U.S. Two-thirds of our 40,000 employees are outside the U.S., as are two-thirds of our 160 manufacturing plants. In all, we operate in 140 nations and have a manufacturing presence in 65.

Throughout all of Pfizer's worldwide operations, there are roughly 75 employees working elsewhere than in their own countries—75 out of 40,000. Fewer than half of those 75 are Americans.

FROM INTERNATIONAL TRADE TO A GLOBAL ECONOMY

Pfizer has changed tremendously in the past four decades. In 1946, Pfizer was still principally a respected fine chemicals company operating almost exclusively within the United States. Today, it is a multinational company, manufacturing and marketing a wide spectrum of products in every part of the world.

Early in this century, the French poet Charles Peguy offered the thought that "it takes time to change a world, but time is all it takes." In the case of the pharmaceutical industry, it took remarkably little time to change drastically the world—metaphorically and literally—in which we operate. Let me begin by citing two examples from our operations within the United States.

Pfizer hired its first full-time attorney on January 2, 1941—92 years after the company's founding. Today, government regulations and the prospect of time-consuming lawsuits force us to consult house attorneys at virtually every turn.

The second change is equally dramatic. Terramycin received FDA approval in March 1950; the patent was granted four months later. The *entire* development and approval process for Terramycin—recovery, purification, animal studies, clinical testing, patenting, and marketing approval—was completed in roughly *one year*. Each decade since has brought additional delays, so that today the development and approval process for a new drug runs *seven to ten* years and consumes an average of $125 million!

Yet as considerable as has been the change in domestic operations, the past four decades have wrought changes even more profound in international commercial relationships. Some of these changes are reflected in statistical comparisons of this and earlier decades.

By any measure, the world has grown more cosmopolitan and, in the current phase, "interdependent." For example, in 1950, 676,000 U.S. citizens traveled to foreign countries. Three and a half decades later the number exceeds 10 million annually. Even more considerable has been the growth of foreign visitors to the U.S.—from 242,000 in 1950 to more than 8 million in the mid-1980s.

Changes in economic figures have been equally impressive. In 1950, the United States exported $57.5 billion (in 1983 dollars); in 1983, U.S. exports were $332.2 billion. The United States imported about $50 billion worth of goods and services in 1950 (in 1983 dollars), and in excess of *seven times* that amount in 1983.

In 1983, the value of U.S.-owned assets abroad was $887 billion, nearly a 400 percent increase since 1950. And the value of U.S. assets held by foreigners increased in the same period from $72.8 billion to $782 billion, an increase of nearly 1,100 percent.

Yet such statistics, dramatic as they are, constitute a mere fraction of the story. For the past four decades have witnessed not only a dramatic increase in international economic activity, but—more importantly—a dramatic change in the nature of the international economic scene.

In the past several decades, there has developed—for the first time in world history—a truly *global* economy. Of course, "international trade" existed even before the Phoenicians. And Venice's centuries-long prosperity was based on "international trade." There are dozens more examples. Yet the global marketplace is something quite different. Peter Drucker explained the difference in his book, *The Age of Discontinuity*, which he wrote nearly 20 years ago:

> If an economy is identified as a common demand pattern, it is also a pool of shared information....The world "information explosion" contributes to making the whole world one economy.
>
> This world economy differs in essentials from the "international economy" that first emerged in the eighteenth century and had, by 1900, become dominant almost everywhere. In an international economy there are no common appetites, no common demands, and only a minimum of common information. Each country in an international economy is a separate unit with its own economic values and preferences, its own markets, and its own largely self-contained information.

As Professor Drucker goes on to explain, all the European countries, prior to World War II, were involved in "international trade," including trade with each other. Yet there were great differences among the peoples of one nation and another, even a neighboring nation. Houses, clothes, food were all different. Travelers carried guidebooks full of observations about each country's preferences.

In the 1980s, when we watch television news, what do we see? We see pictures of Filipinos in one story, and Chileans in the next; the third story is beamed from Italy, the fourth from Indiana, U.S.A. With minor variations, all of the people are wearing the same style of clothing!

This is the most apparent manifestation of an even more fundamental change: by and large, consumers worldwide now seek the same sorts of goods and services. And they know what is available elsewhere, because they have seen and heard about the items via one or another medium of the global information revolution—television, newsmagazines, and the like.

How does this differ from past expansions of trade? Historically, producers and governments pioneered new trading areas. For example, *first* Queen Elizabeth I granted title to a piece of wilderness, *later* (perhaps decades later) the owner of the now-cultivated land sent products back to England and received from England what he needed—that is, trade was begun.

Or, in an example Professor Drucker uses, for decades before significant trade developed, the Western areas of the United States were territories. Political action or imagination preceded trade.

Compare this with Professor Drucker's description of the development in recent decades of the global marketplace:

> Today's world economy, however, owes almost nothing to political imagination. It is coming into being despite political fragmentation. The demands, the appetites, the values are preceding, by a good margin, even the creation of trading units. Indeed, the European Common Market was a belated institutional acknowledgment of what had become the reality of economic perception and of consumer behavior a good many years earlier.
>
> [In the past], producers—with the help of governments, as a rule—created economic units. Consumers played no role, were indeed (as in the early years of the United States) opposed, or at best lukewarm. The new world economy is, by contrast, an achievement of the consumer....
>
> This, then, is a world economy in its demands. But there are, so far, no world economic institutions. There are, therefore, no instruments for a world economic policy, no tools to prevent or fight world economic crises.

In the years since Professor Drucker wrote this passage, many governments have joined in taking some steps to respond positively to the unique global economy that has emerged in the past several decades. Nevertheless, compared with the task of freeing the world's producers to meet the global demand for goods and services—and making economies grow, so people everywhere can afford the products they desire—very little progress has been made.

My reason for describing at length the creation of a global economy is this: without grasping the fact of a global marketplace one cannot grasp the predicament of the multinational corporations.

Corporations such as Pfizer were the first institutions to respond to the global demand for products. Many of the problems I and my colleagues at Pfizer confront each day originate in the inability or unwillingness of governments worldwide to adjust to this new and historically unique global marketplace.

Indeed, when you consider post-World War II currency shortages—such as Pfizer faced when attempting to meet the international demand for antibiotics—and the requirement that companies manufacture locally to sell locally, you will realize that even the very structure of the multinational corporation has been profoundly influenced by governments' tardiness in adjusting to the reality of the global marketplace.

OBSTACLES IN GOVERNMENT POLICIES

Let us now turn to some of the obstacles Pfizer employees confront as members of a high-technology, highly regulated company operating around the globe. To simplify matters, I will discuss only those that relate in some way to governmental policies. I will further divide the issues into those that are the direct effects of governmental policies (for example, drug-approval regulations or barriers to market entry), and those not directly intended by, or only indirectly caused by, governmental policy (for example, currency fluctuation or "intellectual property" issues). In each case, I will mention some of the steps the company has taken to adjust to—or alter—the situation.

By limiting the discussion in this way, I do not mean to suggest that the only difficulties we face are governmentally imposed or influenced. Far from it. For one thing, disease is too cunning and resilient for that, and nature too successful at disguises—as our researchers will be happy to tell you. We have production worries and challenges, as does every industry, and many that are specific to the pharmaceutical industry. There are marketing challenges as well, including preferences peculiar to different markets. (For example, Americans want sweet-tasting medicine; Germans prefer a tart, lemon taste.) Yet a large proportion of the difficulties we face are government-related. By focusing on those sorts of problems, I will be able to paint the broadest canvas in the shortest time.

The New-Drug Approval Process in the U.S.A.

The United States constitutes the world's largest market for pharmaceuticals. U.S.-based companies sell roughly 74 percent of the pharmaceuticals sold in the U.S. market, but U.S.-based companies' share of the U.S. market *and* of the world market has been declining in the past decade.

One reason for this state of affairs is the fact that the United States' drug-approval process is among the longest in the world: on average, nearly three years. Because the full development and approval process for a new drug can take from seven to ten years, the effective life of pharmaceutical patents in the United States has been halved. Recently, a partial remedy, supported by Pfizer and other pharmaceutical companies, was passed by Congress. It extends patent coverage for pharmaceuticals for up to an additional five years to compensate for the length of regulatory review.

Generic Drugs and Future Research

One cost-cutting method used increasingly in recent years has been the substitution of "generic" for "brand-name" drugs whose patents have expired. Drug substitution, in the form of generics, has been growing at a rapid pace in the United States.

The long-term effects of the policy of encouraging generic substitution could be to restrict severely U.S. pharmaceutical companies' ability to finance the research needed to discover and develop new life-saving and life-enhancing drugs.

The U.S.-based pharmaceutical industry spends over $4.5 billion annually on research and development. This research is financed by the sale of innovative brand-name drugs. Four-fifths of the top selling brand-name drugs in 1987 will lose their patent protection in the next four years. Within three years of their patents' expiration, their sales will drop by an average of 50 percent due to competition from generics.

Cost Containment

Throughout the developed nations during the past four decades, and especially since the mid-1960s, there has been a growing trend toward indirect, or third-party, payment of medical bills. A growing share of health costs has been assumed by government programs, such as Medicare and Medicaid in the United States. This trend gives government officials immediate and direct interests in lowering health care costs. Unfortunately, government programs have sometimes achieved savings by opting for the least expensive, but not the most cost-effective, forms of treatment: a "penny-wise, pound-foolish" approach. If a cheaper prosthetic implant, for example, necessitated additional repeat surgery, the net effect would be to spend more money, not less—because of the extra surgery involved.

Because so many hospitals are increasingly dependent on government monies, their administrators also face incentives to cut costs in the short term, without regard for the long-term consequences for the quality of health care. Yet, overly stringent cost-containment measures have the potential to affect health care quality in the long run, by interfering in the doctor-patient relationship, reducing the number and kinds of new drugs and treatments available to patients, and reducing funds for research and innovation in the health field.

Other U.S. Policy Problems

There has been much concern in recent years about trade and the competitiveness of U.S. firms in the global marketplace. Unfortunately, some facts about trade have not enjoyed the attention they deserve. For example, very few people realize that roughly 80 percent of all manufactured U.S. export goods are products of multinational companies, or that approximately 40 percent of all U.S. manufactured goods are exported to the foreign-owned subsidiaries of U.S. companies.

Despite recent concerns, precious little has been done to alleviate the systemic impediments to competitiveness

(though U.S. efforts to curb unfair practices by foreign governments has improved dramatically). Several policy areas are
greatly in need of reform:

- U.S. fiscal policy, especially our huge deficit, continues to
  hamper business by considerably increasing the cost of
  capital.
- Our export administration laws and antitrust laws also
  dampen the ability of U.S.-based firms to compete abroad.
- Our tax policy has rarely been so much as examined with
  an eye to its competitive effects.
- Our legal system cries for reform of tort law. Millions of
  dollars are spent each year by companies of every size and
  description, including Pfizer, fighting off attorneys intent
  on playing "bingo" with the law.
- Hostile takeovers have sapped the resources of some U.S.
  companies and diverted management attention from
  pursuing long-range goals and objectives. Our securities
  laws need to be amended to provide a "level playing field"
  for hostile-takeover battles and to prevent the abusive
  practices of corporate raiders, who are usually only interested in making enormous personal profits by "putting
  companies in play."

Abroad, A Regulatory Challenge

Between multinational pharmaceutical companies and the
consumers who need their products, sit some 160 governments
of the world, each with its own sets of regulations, government
agencies, boards of approval, and motives generous or base. To
manage a multinational company at any level is to spend a
sizable portion of one's time complying with governmental
regulations. To head a company with subsidiaries and sales
throughout the globe is to learn at first hand the universality of
human imperfection and the multitude of ways to skin a cat.
Unfortunately, the cat is usually yours. And increasingly so in a
world where more and more governments try to cope with the
cost pressures of their health-care systems. It is a fact that
throughout the world there are precious few national health-
care systems that operate on a free-market basis. Even, or

oftentimes especially, among the industrial democracies, we find a complex of subsidies, which government can afford less and less. Hospitals, doctors, pharmacists, and the pharmaceutical manufacturers are all asked to do their share to reduce health budgets. From the United Kingdom to Bangladesh, Canada to Argentina, West Germany to Nigeria, we find, increasingly, there are pressures to reduce costs. However well-intentioned, such pressures make it more and more difficult to fund the necessary R&D for the medicines of the future. It is a serious commercial, policy, and moral dilemma.

Allow me a few examples of the ways the pharmaceutical industry gets squeezed in the process.

• *price controls:* Since the earliest days of Pfizer's international sales efforts, the prices of our products have been controlled by governmental regulation in numerous countries. This remains the case today; it "goes with the territory."

In recent years, the Japanese have provided the most dramatic example: a policy of directly reducing prices. In the early to mid-1980s, the Japanese government undertook substantial price reductions for all pharmaceutical products sold in their country, in order to reduce medical costs, which in Japan are mainly subsidized by the government. Other governments utilize more subtle means to reach a similar end. The United Kingdom controls profits by restricting return on investment according to a complex formula. France simply freezes prices from time to time. Other countries restrict profits by altering the list of which drugs can and cannot be reimbursed under their national health-care schemes.

• *limits on direct investment:* Because we manufacture and sell throughout the world, investment issues—the ability to invest and operate in countries without being discriminated against—are extremely important to us. But investment issues are also important to the countries in which we operate. It is through direct investment that the multinational corporation has contributed most substantially to economic growth and technological development around the world. All the more so in the case of the pharmaceutical industry, where the economic and techno-logical advances lead to transfers of knowledge about medicine. Increased life spans and enormous improve-ments in the quality of life have spread from the U.S. through Western Europe, to Asia and throughout the developing world. The pharmaceutical multinational cor-poration has contributed to these improved conditions through its direct investment and the accompanying benefits. From this perspective, it is puzzling that many of the countries most in need of direct investment have policies that adversely affect the very companies whose presence means increased knowledge, technology, and commerce.

Many countries insist, for example, that you manufac-ture locally. Furthermore, some governments insist that a certain percentage of all goods produced by exported. These and similar requirements can distort local economies.

For the developing nations of the world, few things are more short-sighted than the hobbling of foreign invest-ment. Yet it is a common practice. Year after year, it counteracts the leavening power of trade, and exacts a toll in unnecessary poverty and suffering.

Pfizer and many other companies have gone to great effort in the past several years to explain this to the U.S. and other governments. We have sought to expand their understanding of "trade" issues to include discrimination against direct investment by foreign firms. We have worked to have direct investment included as a topic in the current round of GATT (General Agreement on Tariffs and Trade) talks. The relaxation of restrictions on foreign direct investment is vital to the growth of the world economy, as well as the individual economies of develop-ing nations.

With governments throughout the world major players in the global marketplace, a multinational company is also indirectly affected by governmental policies in myriad ways. Let me men-tion merely two difficulties.

Currency Fluctuation

We often hear on television newscasts and elsewhere "the dollar closed today" up or down, by this or that amount. Many people admit to finding such pronouncements rather mysterious. Those of us who work for multinational corporations have learned their meaning from experience, some of it hard-won. Because we manufacture and sell all over the world, Pfizer has dealings in nearly every currency on the face of the earth!

In 1980, when the value of the dollar was relatively low in relation to other currencies, 57 percent of Pfizer's sales were made outside the United States. By 1985, sales abroad accounted for only 40 percent of our total sales, in part because of the dollar's increased strength. This phenomenon had an obviously negative impact on our reported sales. In fact, we estimate that, from 1983 to 1985, Pfizer's reported sales were $400 million lower because of the effect of the strong dollar on currency translations. More recently, the situation has improved significantly, due to the decline in the value of the dollar.

The overall currency situation dramatizes both the potential volatility of currency values and the problems those uncertainties pose for multinationals. Clearly, given our choice, we would prefer an international environment in which exchange rates—whatever their level—were reasonably stable.

Protecting "Intellectual Property"

This brings us to the vitally important issue of protecting "intellectual property."

What is "intellectual property?" That's simple; in fact, you already know the answer. It's just that you usually think of it in terms of its protection—a patent, trademark, or copyright.

"Intellectual property" involves the right of the discoverer of an innovation, product, or process—or the creator of a work, such as a writer of books or computer software—to utilize it, including profit from it, as he or she sees fit, and more particularly to preclude its unauthorized use by others. This exclusive right to the product of one's own labors and creativity is generally granted for a fixed period of years (in the case of patents, for example, for 17 years).

In agreeing to the Paris Convention in the 19th century, and thereby recognizing "intellectual property," the international community sought to create incentives to discovery. The idea was to ensure direct benefit from the discovery and to ensure that one could recoup the research and development costs. The whole world benefits from the rapid dissemination of new information that intellectual property protection makes possible—for example, by the early disclosure of inventions in patents.

So what's the problem? Well, not all countries, much less all business firms abroad, respect intellectual property. Outside the small community of industrial democracies—the U.S., the West European nations, Australia, and Japan—there is in fact precious little respect for intellectual property rights. (Not coincidentally, the nations that lead the world in respect for property—whether "intellectual" or other forms of property— also lead the world in economic and technological development.) Around the world, companies with discoveries and innovative technologies to protect through patents, copyrights, trademarks, and trade secrets, time and again have failed to thwart the theft of these valuable properties. High-technology firms such as Pfizer regularly find that foreign competitors have appropriated innovations without permission or payment.

The disregard of intellectual property rights has been most common in newly industrialized nations and in most developing countries. In some countries, entire domestic industries have been built around pirated U.S. technology and counterfeited goods.

Pharmaceutical companies are precisely the kind of targets attractive to international pirates and their likes. Our manufacturing costs are relatively low, whereas our research and development costs in money and time (which is what the pirate wants principally to avoid by his theft) are quite high. It costs an average of $125 million dollars to bring a new product to market, and up to ten years. Yet in a country without any effective patent protection, a trained chemist can easily duplicate one of our products, and manufacture it in sufficient quantities to preempt the market for our drug.

Pfizer's anti-arthritic drug, Feldene, introduced in the early

1980s, provides a disturbing example. By the time we got Feldene on the market in Argentina, we found we had a local, generic competitor—someone who had confiscated our invention without our permission or payment to us. By the end of the first year Feldene was on the market in Argentina, there were four pirated local generic versions competing with our product. Today, we face competition from some 24 pirated brands.

Complicating matters still further, in most countries laws actually do exist to provide for protection of intellectual property. However, they are either wholly inadequate in light of the realities of selling a product—as in India, where the term is so short that the patent runs out before a product can be brought to market—or the laws simply are not enforced. The latter is true in Argentina, for instance, where the government can point to the existence of laws, but where they are, in the event, flagrantly disregarded by government and private citizen alike. Or, in Canada, where the compulsory licensing provisions effectively undercut any real patent protection in the pharmaceutical and food industries. (Though Canada is seeking to amend its law, the changes would still leave Canadian law far short of providing the adequate protection appropriate to an industrial democracy of its stature.)

Pfizer is only one of hundreds of U.S. companies victimized by piracy of products and processes, and the pharmaceutical industry only one of scores of industries. The U.S. copyright industries (including entertainment and publishing) estimate that because ten newly industrialized countries have failed to provide adequate copyright protection, the U.S. industries lose $1.3 billion in annual sales. (The ten countries are Singapore, Taiwan, Indonesia, Korea, the Philippines, Malaysia, Thailand, Brazil, Egypt, and Nigeria.)

Unfortunately, losses resulting from the pirating of intellectual property are not one-time misfortunes. Usually, these lost sales reflect lost *markets*. And markets, once lost, are difficult indeed to recover.

The price and cost undercutting that result from piracy of patents, trademarks, and copyrights rob companies such as Pfizer of our foremost competitive advantage, our technology. Our technological innovations are our best competitive edge.

Furthermore, since piracy precludes our recovering past R & D funds, our ability to compete in the global marketplace is directly tied to our ability to protect our patented and copyrighted technologies. As important, it robs the citizen of the country of the benefits of the technology, education, and economic advancement that would otherwise take place.

What is Pfizer doing to extend protection of intellectual property? First of all, we have worked tirelessly to explain to the U.S. and other sympathetic governments the necessity of tying the issue of intellectual property rights to discussions of trade. The present international intellectual property treaties have no enforcement or dispute-resolution procedures, and there is no way within those conventions themselves to bring pressure on an offending country to correct the abuses. Thus it is essential that we tie protection of intellectual property to trade issues.

Acting both multilaterally and bilaterally, the U.S. government has led the fight for fair treatment of businesses in the global marketplace—including for protection of their intellectual property. In fact, being part of this process has been one of the most heartening experiences of my business life. And let me stress this often-neglected point: since a certain degree of trust is necessary for markets to function, fair treatment for all parties is not an effort of national interest alone, but also one of genuine international consequence.

Pfizer and other companies pushed hard to assure that intellectual property issues would be scheduled for discussion at the latest round of the multilateral GATT talks, the first session of which was held in September 1986 in Uruguay. We want GATT to authorize using market access as leverage to obtain better patent, copyright, trademark, and trade-secret protection, and to encourage adoption of fundamental principles of intellectual property protection by all nations. (Several business leaders, myself included, accompanied the U.S. delegation, in order to provide on-the-scene advice on key business issues.)

Bilateral efforts have also shown promise. In 1984, the Congress amended the definition of an unfair trade barrier to include the refusal to protect intellectual property. Consequently, in one recent case involving South Korea, U.S. negotiators were able to tie U.S.-market access for South Korean exports to better intellectual property protection for U.S. products in South Korea.

In another action that will be resolved bilaterally, the U.S. Pharmaceutical Manufacturers Association recently brought a complaint with the U.S. government against the government of Brazil. Some years ago, Brazil rewrote its patent law to totally exclude pharmaceuticals from protection! Indeed, according to Brazilian law, it is perfectly all right for Brazilian businesses to use the discoveries of foreign pharmaceutical companies without paying for them. This policy has cost American-based pharmaceutical firms more than $160 million since 1979, and probably a billion more in lost opportunity.

In recent years, the U.S. government and U.S.-based multinationals have cooperated closely in efforts to open world markets, to break down barriers to international investment, and to bolster the protection of intellectual property.

BEYOND THE OBSTACLES

Charles Pfizer and Charles Erhart died long before I was born. When Pfizer scientists, working around-the-clock, discovered at last a way to mass produce penicillin, thus saving the lives of countless Allied soldiers, I was still in high school. Terramycin was brought to market, and the foundation of Pfizer's worldwide operations was cemented, in the decade before I joined the company. Thus, although I have known personally many of Pfizer's management and research pioneers, many others, who were before my time, I will never have the pleasure of knowing. Yet I can say with assurance that those who created Pfizer, those who helped develop it, and those who now nurture its growth, hold in common beliefs about the value of work, the excitement of scientific discovery, and the ability to improve human life by the application of intellect.

Dr. An Wang, the remarkable founder of Wang Laboratories, recently published his autobiography. His closing words beautifully express the gratification that comes of applying one's mind and energy to the improvement of life. Dr. Wang wrote, "The satisfaction of turning an idea into something real never diminishes, and the great gift of change is that it continually replenishes the stock of new ideas that might be brought to life."

Unfortunately, as I hope I have demonstrated in the preceding pages, between the discoverers and producers of pharmaceuticals and their would-be beneficiaries, there are nowadays countless obstacles. I have concentrated on those caused by governmental action or inertia.

If life were perfect or perfectible, perhaps there would be no regulations. If human beings and their institutions were perfect, there would be no need for regulations.

As it is, there must be some, and there are nowadays too many.

In the years ahead, if the world has a run of luck, there will be fewer hurdles between the first worldwide commercial organizations, the multinational corporations, and the consumers who in recent decades created history's first global marketplace. Such a triumph of good sense would mean, among other things, prosperity for unprecedented numbers of the world's people.

Between that happy condition and our own, there stand three prerequisites. They are indispensable to success in any enterprise. They will be needed by those many national governments and agencies from whom more enlightened policies will be expected in the future. Prudence, to know what might be done. Courage, to do what should be done. Determination, to do what must be done to better life in our time, and to trailblaze a freer, more prosperous world in the century to come.

Tadahiro Sekimoto

Tadahiro Sekimoto was appointed president of the Nippon Electric Company (NEC) in 1980. He was previously executive vice president.

Mr. Sekimoto received a bachelor of science degree in physics from the University of Tokyo in 1948. He completed a doctor of engineering degree, also at the University of Tokyo, in 1962.

Mr. Sekimoto joined NEC in 1948. By 1974, he was associate senior vice president of the firm, and served as a senior vice president from 1974 to 1978. In 1978, he was promoted to president and acting director of subsidiaries.

In 1976, Mr. Sekimoto received the Japanese Government Prize. He accepted the New York State Governor's Award on behalf of NEC in 1985.

A chairman and president of the Business Council, Mr. Sekimoto is also a member of the Institute of Electronics and Communications Engineers of Japan, the Institute of Electrical Engineers of Japan, the Acoustical Society of Japan, and the Japanese Operations Research Society.

7
MEETING THE CHALLENGE
OF THE 21ST CENTURY

Tadahiro Sekimoto
President
NEC Corporation, Japan

C&C GROWS ON A GLOBAL SCALE

We at NEC define ourselves as "a world enterprise leading the way into the 21st century with C&C"—a phrase that encapsulates many of our ideas. First, take "C&C," the integration of computers and communications. NEC introduced this new concept to the world in 1977. It involves the convergence and eventual union of computers and communications, as computers are increasingly linked by communications networks in distributed processing, while communications are increasingly digitalized on the same principle as the computer.

To explain C&C to the layperson, we compare it to an artificial servant. In this comparison, the computer is likened to an artificial brain, communications to artificial nerves, input devices to artificial sense organs (e.g., voice recognition devices serve as ears), output devices such as voice synthesizers to artificial vocal cords, and robots to artificial arms and legs. The artificial cells that make up the "body" are semiconductors and integrated circuits (ICs). (The latter are the "cells" of machines in so many sectors that they have been dubbed the new rice, the new oil of industry.) With every advance in these technologies, the artificial servant will develop a more powerful body.

Of equal importance, however, is the intelligence conferred by software. It is this feature that sets C&C entirely apart from conventional equipment. The intelligence derives, of course, from us, the machines' human masters, and C&C will always remain our servant. The potential is there for "personal" servants designed to meet the particular needs of each of us. But it remains to be seen whether humanity—or, rather, each of us individually—has the wisdom to create and effectively employ these artificial servants.

I visualize C&C on this grand scale because I believe, with Professor Daniel Bell and others, that the new technologies are transforming the very structure of society. The integration of computers and communications and the use of semiconductors and ICs intensify the power of knowledge in what amounts to the biggest breakthrough since the industrial revolution harnessed steam and iron to boost our muscle power. This is why we refer to today's technological innovations as part of a second industrial revolution—the information revolution, or the C&C revolution. The forces now at work are providing the momentum that will lead us to an information society.

These changes are not limited to the United States, nor to Japan. The momentum is global. In a sense C&C has brought us to a turning point in world history. NEC was quick to spot this fact, and we first shared our insights not at home in Japan but at the INTELCOM '77 convention in Atlanta, Georgia. This choice reflects the way in which our role as a C&C company has required us to become a world enterprise.

The question the company has faced has been how best to organize ourselves internally for this purpose. NEC has adopted a range of operations in all four areas basis to C&C: computers, communications, home electronics, and electronic devices. In the coming C&C era, it will be important to maintain a good balance among these areas and to create, through their interaction, a whole which is greater than the sum of its parts. This combination gives NEC a uniquely strong position in the industry. According to one recent survey, NEC's 1985 sales ranked seventh in the world in computers, sixth in communications equipment, and first in electronic devices. We are the only company in the world that is in the top ten in every one of these fields. Thanks to this range of operations, NEC has truly become a world enterprise.

DESTINED TO INTERNATIONALIZE

NEC's management strategies are characterized by four principles: foresight, action, staying power, and flexibility. Success in any venture requires first the foresight to see into the future. But this by itself is not enough. We must be able to translate our insights into realities—to take action. However, business is not as simple as that. There is stiff competition from other companies, and only rarely can a goal be attained at once. Naturally, then, we need the staying power to persist in our efforts over the long term. Yet it is just as important to be flexible, to be able to adjust quickly when changes in business conditions make the initial goal inappropriate. This is the kind of flexibility suggested by the saying, "A wise man knows when to change his mind."

The history of NEC's overseas operations demonstrates how effectively these four principles have been applied. NEC, established on July 17, 1899, was destined from the outset to expand overseas, for as a manufacturer of communications equipment, its operations would inevitably reach beyond national boundaries. As humanity has pushed the limits of its sphere of activity ever outwards—developing transport systems on the seas and in the air—communications systems have also had to expand over the globe to serve them. This was where NEC came in. It was the first joint-venture company set up in Japan by a U.S.-Japan partnership, with 54 percent of its capital supplied by Western Electric (now AT&T Technologies, Inc.). Though the capital relationship no longer exists today, NEC was the first tangible case of Japan-U.S. economic cooperation.

At the end of World War II, Japan chose an export-based economic policy to help rebuild the war-torn economy. This was a crucial step for the survival of 100 million people in a small country with no natural resources to speak of. NEC was then becoming increasingly interested in extending its operations overseas, in light of these conditions and the essentially international nature of its own business. In fact, even before the period of postwar chaos had ended, the company's Tamagawa factory had set itself the goal of becoming the world's number-one plant. This was a clear manifestation of the foresight that recognized the importance of doing business overseas. And in the late 1950s NEC began to fulfill this longstanding desire to develop international business activities of its own.

Foresight must be acted upon. In the world market for communications equipment in the 1950s, however, American and European manufacturers had built up a strong record of exports to the developing nations that were the major customers; they had established a dominant business base in these countries through their local plants and the communications operating services they provided. This made things extremely difficult for newcomers. It required a concentrated company-wide effort for us to penetrate these markets, and to achieve growing sales in them. Around 1958, for example, international bids were opened for a microwave communications route linking Turkey, Iran and Pakistan. Our company placed a bid, but the contract was initially awarded to an American radio equipment manufacturer which had offered a very low price. This company ran into problems with the technical specifications, however, and it was NEC that supplied the system in the end. The experience taught us that success in the international market depends on factors other than pricing. A company needs overall capabilities from the planning stage to post-installation maintenance, and the capacity to set high standards that will convince the customer. The importance of action and staying power—not giving up too easily, not yielding to the competition—was another lesson we learned on this occasion.

We were first induced to think about technology transfer when we were negotiating to export television broadcasting equipment to India in 1960. The Indian side insisted that we hand over the manufacturing know-how, which they would then use to export products in competition with NEC. As India had a strong influence on its neighbors and was a particularly promising market, we finally accepted their arguments and agreed to supply the technology. During these negotiations we became keenly aware that we could never rest content with our existing technology, that without the foresight to pursue the potential of new technology, we would lose our viability for the future. If we are to grow tomorrow, it is no good holding onto the technology we possess today. The export of technology can be successful only when the company has technology a step or two in advance of what it exports. To become a world enterprise, we learned, we must be able to undertake a certain amount of technology transfer as part of our international business and still make our operations profitable.

The growth of exports also brought demands for local production. In 1958 NEC set up its first postwar joint-venture company in Taiwan to manufacture telephone switching equipment. Here again we gained valuable experience in international operations. With the backing of the Taiwanese government, we initially concluded a tie-up with a local commercial partner, but the relationship foundered, since this partner preferred to go after short-term profits. We later switched to an industrial partner with much better success. This taught us that careful consideration must be given, before entering a joint-venture partnership, to the partner's approach to management and to the nature of the company itself. The experience also brought home to us the need to be flexible, to correct mistakes as soon as they are recognized.

THE FOUR MANAGEMENT PRINCIPLES IN PRACTICE

For NEC the 1950s were a decade of study and of laying the groundwork for our international operations. In the 1960s we were finally ready to take on full-scale export activities. The time had come to test our ability to act. The time had also come to put our four basic business areas (computers, communications, home electronics, and electronic devices) and our four management principles (foresight, action, staying power, and flexibility) to work internationally. The Japanese economy was just entering a period of unprecedented rapid growth as a result of government policy, and exports were growing at a similarly rapid rate. However, the recession that began in 1964 caused a marked slowdown in domestic demand, while on the international scene the United States strengthened its policy of defending the dollar, making competition on international markets extremely intense. Nevertheless, NEC's export sales continued to expand steadily. Our export lines included radio and telephone switching equipment and color TVs, and our markets now extended beyond Southeast Asia into the Middle and Near East, the Pacific islands, and Latin America.

In the 1960s we created a production and marketing network overseas by opening a series of representative offices and other commercial bases in major cities around the world. In 1963 we established a sales company in the United States. Nippon Electric New York, which then occupied just one room of Manhattan's Pan Am Building, has grown today into NEC America, Inc.

By the late 1960s we began to think about full-scale local production. We established local production firms for communications equipment in Mexico and Brazil (1968) and Australia (1969), and today they are important production facilities in each of these countries. Yet, however necessary it may be, the transfer of operations overseas is no easy job. Only when a company integrates locally with a long-term perspective and sufficient practical experience can it hope to set its operations on a sure footing. Staying power is a must for lasting success.

August 1971 brought the "dollar shock." A steep rise in the value of the yen and the shift to a floating exchange rate system seriously worsened the export climate. Before Japanese industry had a chance to recover, the oil shock of autumn 1973 triggered rampant inflation, and the tight money policies designed to control this led to a severe recession. These two events shook the very framework of the postwar world economy. All over the globe efforts began to establish a new economic order. Though this was a time that put every company's staying power and flexibility to the test, NEC pressed on to consolidate its base as a world enterprise. Although the two shocks certainly had a serious impact on NEC's business, we had fortunately already established a solid record of sales in many countries, and our products had earned a high reputation for quality and reliability around the world. Furthermore, as the oil-producing nations began to spend their increased revenues to improve their social infrastructure (communications systems, etc.), our export markets—especially in the Middle East—actually began to expand in spite of the overall worsening of the export climate. The benefits of this were soon offset, however, by the rapid appreciation of the yen. Valued at Y 293 to the dollar in January 1977, by October 1978 the yen had broken the Y 180 barrier. As a result, our exports leveled off in fiscal 1977 and 1978 after having climbed year after year. Even so, technological innovations such as the striking advances in semiconductor and IC technology and the digitalization of communications created new business opportunities, and we launched electronic devices and digital switching equipment on the world market as new strategic products.

We also stepped up our overseas representation during the 1970s. In the communications field, we set up PERNAS NEC Multiplex as a joint venture in 1973, while in computers we created NEC Computers Singapore in 1977. In the field of home electronics, we began local production of color TVs by joint ventures in South Korea (1970) and Australia (1974), and our 1979 investment in an Argentinian company strengthened our production in Central and South America.

During this period, we set up production and marketing facilities for electronic devices. To beat the intense competition in this growth industry, we needed a farsighted marketing strategy based on a knowledge of world demand. Accordingly, we planned and established our production and sales network from the perspective of a world enterprise after studying such questions as local policies to attract business, labor, import tariffs and quotas, and after conducting in-depth surveys of market trends in various countries. In rapid succession we founded NEC Ireland Ltd. (1974) as a semiconductor and IC production base for the EC region; NEC Malaysia Sdn. Berhad (1974) to produce semiconductors for Southeast Asia; and NEC Singapore Pte., Ltd. (1976) to produce and market display devices. Then in 1978 we acquired Electronic Arrays Inc., a middle-ranked American manufacturer, as a step toward producing electronic devices locally in the United States.

TOWARD A WORLD ENTERPRISE

Following on the turbulent '70s, the 1980s have been years in which NEC has really developed its operations as a world enterprise. Our flexible response to change has proved effective in product development and marketing strategies. Our international sales have climbed again, accounting for a share of our total sales which has now topped 30 percent. In Asia and the Pacific, we established NEC Information Systems Australia in 1981 and, in the same year, renamed PERNAS NEC Multiplex and consolidated its structure as PERNAS NEC Telecommunication. Also in 1981, we set up NEC Semiconductors UK as our second production base in the Western European region and reorganized our European marketing system. In the U.S. as well, we reorganized our local network and combined the existing three companies into one, NEC Electronics U.S.A., Inc., for a consolidated manufacturing and marketing structure.

Now let us take a closer look at NEC's presence in the U.S., where we now employ over 5,000 people. First, in the field of communications equipment, NEC America, Inc. has five factories on American soil (in Dallas, Texas; Hillsboro, Oregon; Fairfax, Virginia; Melville, New York; and Hawthorne, California) as well as over twenty direct sales outlets. We supply product clusters—switching equipment for public telephone exchanges, communications terminal equipment, satellite communications equipment, fiber optics communications systems, and others—in a truly close relationship with our clients and the marketplace. Our wide spectrum of clients includes the regional holding companies formed after AT&T's divestiture in 1984.

In the computer field, we established NEC Systems Laboratories, Inc., in 1972 just outside Boston, Massachusetts, the mecca of the U.S. computer industry, and launched our own market surveys and research. In 1977 we set up NEC Information Systems, Inc., a manufacturing and sales company for data processing equipment. And 1984 saw the construction of a new plant as part of a concentration on improving our facilities for the local manufacture and supply of all kinds of data processing equipment, especially the small office computers, personal computers and printers that make up the core of office automation systems.

In the field of electronic devices, we established NEC Microcomputers, Inc., an IC sales company, near Boston in 1975, and in 1978 we bought Electronic Arrays, Inc., in California's Silicon Valley, the hub of the U.S. semiconductor industry. In 1979 we added NEC Electron to the list. By 1981, when these three sales and production companies were firmly established, we unified their operations in the central Silicon Valley under the name NEC Electronics U.S.A., Inc. To further reinforce our capacity for local manufacture of semiconductor products, we built a new plant in 1984 outside Sacramento, California, and created an operation whose integrated production system includes everything from the key process of forming electronic circuits on silicon wafers to putting the last touches on the finished product.

In the field of home electronics, we split off the home electronics division of NEC America, Inc., in 1982 and an independent company, NEC Home Electronics (USA), Inc., located in suburban Chicago. This strengthened our sales capacity for a cluster of products centered around television and audio equipment and personal computers for home use. In 1985 this company opened a plant near Atlanta, Georgia, and commenced production of television sets and other product lines.

As a result of similar efforts toward internationalization and globalization of our operations in numerous countries, NEC has grown by 1988 into a truly world enterprise. We have dealings in 144 countries, 26 offices in 25 countries, 23 sales companies in 14 countries, 20 production companies and 24 plants in 13 countries, and a total of 17,500 overseas employees.

As NEC celebrated its 88th anniversary in 1987, we looked back with pride on our history of postwar international business activities. In the 1950s we laid the foundation for overseas activities, in the 60s we entered international markets chiefly as an exporter, in the 70s we gained a footing as an international firm, and in the 80s we developed our operations as a world enterprise. It is a history of difficulties overcome, and it is a productive history.

After almost 40 years we are at last beginning to draw attention in the international marketplace and are now able to give
leadership to companies and experts around the world in
proclaiming the concept of C&C. During this time, foresight
and action combined with staying power to withstand hard
times and the flexibility to adapt to change have been the keys
to management success. On the solid foundation of these
attributes, the NEC Group as a whole has attained sales of 2.33
trillion yen ($13.1 billion in fiscal 1986) and a total of 96,000
employees.

A BUSINESS IS ONLY AS GOOD AS ITS STAFF—A GLOBAL BUSINESS IS ONLY AS GOOD AS ITS WORLDWIDE STAFF

What factors lie behind this growth of NEC's overseas
operations? A number of answers come to mind, but I would
like to concentrate here on a few key points. First, there is our
overall management stance, which I have already discussed in
terms of foresight, action, staying power, and flexibility.

Second, there is our commitment to offering better products
and better services. This was taught us by our partner, Western
Electric, at the time of NEC's inception. In following this
philosophy NEC has learned many lessons. One is the importance of research and development. Electronics has always
been a very fast-moving technology, and in recent years
progress has accelerated still further until we are now seeing a
worldwide technological development race. The classic example is semiconductors and ICs. Consider memory capacity,
for example. In 1973 a prototype was developed with a 1 K
(1,024 bit) memory. Two years later IC memories could handle
4 K; in another two years, 16 K; in another two years, 64 K. Then
following a 256 K stage, memory capacity reached an astonish-
ing 1 M (1 million bits) in 1985. In other words, performance
has quadrupled every two years. To fall behind in this development race is to lose the ability to make good products and good
artificial servants. Not only would this dash the company's
hopes of becoming a world enterprise, but the very survival of
its operations would be threatened.

Another key point involves the importance of a market-oriented approach to the achievement of better products and better services. Products must vary between different countries and different cultures. Good products and services are those which respect and comply with the consumers' needs. An example is the built-in word-processing function of personal computers: unless a product to be used in China can process Chinese, it can hardly claim to be suited for the Chinese market. Products will also be used under widely varying climatic conditions. Unless their reliability is geared to local conditions, NEC products will not be popular. Naturally, good quality control plays an important role. That is why NEC and other Japanese makers have been able, in spite of our slow start, to expand our semiconductor and IC business worldwide. We ourselves used to import quantities of American-made semiconductors, but when we incorporated them in products and shipped them to clients, we received a significant number of complaints about quality. This was a major problem for us, one which challenged our credibility. We took a series of corrective measures and eventually increased our ability to supply our own electronics devices. When U.S.-Japan trade frictions arose in the semiconductor industry, Hewlett-Packard, having had similar experiences in the U.S., presented statistics on the superior quality of Japanese products. This again brought home to us the value of a market-oriented approach. I have always said that "Sales are the provision of satisfaction, and maintenance service is the provision of continuing satisfaction." With this motto we are attempting to incorporate a market-oriented approach company-wide.

Third comes the training of personnel. It is often said that a business is only as good as its staff, and the same goes for the internationalization or globalization of a business. We therefore maintain a large number of personnel programs for internationalization with our international training program at the core. This involves three focal areas: (1) the training of international business people; (2) the training of personnel for overseas assignments; and (3) the training of local managers.

The actual curriculum begins with language courses. English-language training is divided into skill areas such as conversation, writing, and presentation giving. Instruction is also available in Spanish, Portuguese, French, Chinese, and a number of other languages. Next come courses on various aspects of business administration. These include international law, international accounting, international personnel management, international production systems, and international marketing, as well as courses on related subjects such as trading procedures, international finance, and international insurance.

A special feature is the training given to employees' spouses before they are posted overseas. The experience of the previous appointee's spouse is passed on in detail, person to person, and the wealth of information thus accumulated serves as an asset for the entire company.

We also try to increase opportunities for active contact with other cultures. Our overseas study program is a case in point. We also have a local manager-training program, in which we bring local managers from various countries to Tokyo to give them a better understanding of Japan and NEC. In this connection, the NEC Group holds an annual World Zero Defects (ZD) Convention, in which managers and local supervisors from affiliated companies overseas gather in Tokyo to exchange QC know-how.

BEYOND TRADE FRICTION

NEC is a world enterprise leading the way into the 21st century with C&C. To live up to this description, we need to maintain an all-out effort to solve the problems involved in internationalization and globalization. The problem most frequently encountered is trade friction. Such friction arises basically because of the very intensity of economic contacts. Viewed in this light, it is not something to be deplored, but rather a problem to be considered in a way that will contribute to the mutual advancement of the countries concerned.

NEC has persistently worked toward this end. The most obvious factor here is the character of the products we supply. C&C equipment is the infrastructure on which an information society is built. Exporting C&C equipment and systems is in itself a form of positive economic exchange in many cases.

Second, we can point to our concern for localization. I have already mentioned the localization of products, and we are just as active in localizing our management. We have already appointed many local managers: of NEC's 17,500 overseas employees, only about 3 percent have been sent from Japan. In terms of capital, although in principle we prefer 100 percent equity for greater effectiveness of management, where local circumstances indicate it, we have accepted minority equity participation on a case-by-case basis. We also prefer to use locally procured parts as much as possible after a careful consideration of quality.

Our efforts extend into a third area as well, that of international exchanges. We make sure that the management of our local companies respects the host culture. Even in cases where "Japanese-style" management is called for, we try to ensure that the need is fully understood. One outcome of these "soft" contacts: the British personnel director of NEC Electronics UK holds Parents' Coffee Evenings to show the mothers and fathers of new employees around the plant in an example of personnel management that is essentially Japanese. Conversely, we send young workers from our Japanese plants to NEC Ireland, NEC Electronics, and elsewhere to help promote mutual understanding.

Twenty years ago, I myself spent two years living in the U.S.A. working for an American company. One of the things that struck me at the time was the difference in the way we keep the ball count in baseball: 1-2 means one ball, two strikes in the U.S. and one strike, two balls in Japan. And the Japanese ball is also said to be slightly smaller. Cultural differences arise even in the identical game of baseball, where such things as differences in physical stature can lead to subtle adaptations. Perhaps one of the root causes of trade friction is our failure to understand each other's differences.

When we bought Electronic Arrays, we did an exhaustive study to determine what was behind the quality differences between semiconductors made in the U.S. and Japan. One of the causes proved to be a cultural factor: division of labor has gone further in the U.S. This is entirely natural in a nation where rights and duties are always clearly defined, and it can also be seen as one of the more efficient production methods of industrial societies. But under this system, quality control becomes the job of the QC specialists; the production area's responsibility for quality is limited.

In Japan, on the other hand, although each employee has his or her job description, when necessary he or she can take on a job in a related area. The limits of responsibility are not always clear, but this vagueness can be turned to advantage, resulting in a flexible production system. When QC is required for higher efficiency in the production division, the division's own staff does the job. Perhaps the activities of QC circles have been somewhat overemphasized in explaining the success of this approach, but in any case there is clearly an enormous difference in results when QC is considered the responsibility of the productive division.

Let us consider a specific example: the problem of footwear. Semiconductor and IC manufacturers work in micron units. Tiny dust particles invisible to the eye—even one speck of dust just a micron in diameter—can result in a defective product. It is therefore necessary to banish dust completely from the production floor. The air needs to be ten thousand to one million times purer than that of the average office. Every maker adopts a range of measures to keep dust out. Street clothes cannot be worn on the work floor, for example. At Electronic Arrays, however, workers did not change their shoes. As a result, quality suffered, since they were carrying in dirt from outdoors. But detecting the problem was only half the battle. We were told it was the QC specialists' job to maintain quality, and that it was not customary for Americans to change their shoes. No one in Japan had experienced any resistance to changing shoes in the plant, since we traditionally take off our shoes on entering a home. Perhaps this cultural predispostion of the Japanese might be counted an unfair advantage by those who argue over semiconductor trade friction!

In any case, better products and better services create their own market. Good quality in turn cuts down material wastage due to defects and thus brings down the price. The market responds by beating a path to the manufacturer's door. I'm not blaming the U.S. semiconductor industry's problems on shoes alone, but the fact is that this was a cause of Electronic Arrays' poor showing. Cumulatively, such factors can add up to a trade imbalance. Little differences count. A small difference at the decision level is reflected in a great difference in results.

NEC has been able to gain this experience through transferring operations overseas. I feel sure we will continue to pursue this policy of globalization, because we desire world economic prosperity. Continuing globalization is our basic approach to achieving this. Wherever we go in the world, we would prefer not to sit formally around a square conference table, but to talk across a round table as friends.

A BANNER OF HOPE

There can be no future of economic progress without world peace. Ideally, unnecessary friction should also be kept to a minimum. International cooperation is also essential to the creation of the new form of social organization known as the information society. C&C has major contributions to make in this area. Communication is crucial to the achievement of world peace, but it can be hindered by language barriers, for example. Imagine how an automatic telephone interpreting system would facilitate our understanding of one another. How wonderful it would be to be able to pick up such a telephone and communicate directly with whomever we wanted to talk to at any time, in any place. I believe this is possible using artificial intelligence, voice recognition and synthesizing devices, and high-speed data communications networks—the brain, ears, voice and nerves of the artificial servant. While the system might have trouble conveying fine shades of meaning, or translating creative works, such as fiction and poetry, it shouldn't be impossible to get across the essential points without any misunderstanding. This will not be achieved overnight. Nevertheless, I believe it is our responsibility to pursue such dreams, such hopes, such banners. It is NEC's responsibility to supply such technology as a "world enterprise leading the way into the 21st century."

Colby H. Chandler

Colby H. Chandler, elected chairman and chief executive officer of Eastman Kodak Company in May 1983, began his career with Kodak as a quality control engineer in 1950. In 1960, he was promoted to general supervisor of the technical services staff. A recipient of a Sloane Fellowship in 1962, Mr. Chandler studied at the Massachusetts Institute of Technology and, in July 1963, returned to Kodak. In 1974, he was elected a member of the board of directors and an executive vice president, and by January 1977 was a president of the company. In 1979 and 1980, he also served as general manager of the Photographic Division.

Mr. Chandler earned a B.S. degree in engineering physics from the University of Maine and a master's degree in industrial management from MIT. He holds honorary doctor degrees from Clarkson College, the University of Maine, the State University of New York at Geneseo, Washington and Jefferson University, and Roberts Wesleyan.

A member of several honorary scholastic societies, Mr. Chandler was elected secretary and a governor of the Society of Sloan Fellows in 1964 and served as president of that group from 1966 to 1968. He is a member of the boards of trustees of several institutions, and is on the boards of directors of Ford Motor Company, JCPenney Company, Inc., and Citicorp. In addition to several other civic and professional commitments, Mr. Chandler is a member of the U.S. Corporate Council on South Africa and chairman of the President's Export Council.

8
COMPETITION IN THE WORLD ECONOMY

Colby H. Chandler
Chairman and Chief Executive Officer
Eastman Kodak Company, USA

AN INTERNATIONAL CRISIS

The U.S. faces a trade and international financial crisis of unprecedented proportions in the last half of the 1980s. In a few short years, we have gone from running a virtual balance in our current account to a deficit of roughly $160 billion. From a provider of capital to the rest of the world, we have become the largest debtor. The U.S. manufacturing sector, once considered preeminent, is now under siege. Unless appropriate policy actions are taken soon, we face a grim future of substantially lower standards of living, higher inflation, and slow growth in order to "pay our way" and redress the imbalances that currently exist.

This unhappy vision is not inevitable, however. Much will depend on the policies adopted by the Congress and the administration in the months ahead. To a businessman who depends on open markets and a sound global economy, it seems clear that there are constructive ways to deal with our problems, as well as destructive ones. Which path we take depends on properly identifying the fundamental causes of our problem. Treating symptoms will only exacerbate our troubles in the long run. Above all, we need to avoid politically attractive, short-term solutions. It is very easy to blame others for our problems and devise policies accordingly. However, that will not lead to an expansion of world trade, an improvement in the competitiveness of U.S. business, or a reduction in the trade deficit.

The major causes of our trade deficit and our lack of competitiveness can be found in three broad categories. The first is macroeconomic policy. The second is the debt burden of the developing countries. The third is the fact that much of the rest of the world has, in a very short period, "caught up" with the United States in terms of technology, manufacturing and marketing capabilities.

First, we need to examine the conduct of macroeconomic policy, both in the United States and abroad. We surely cannot reduce the trade deficit and restore American competitiveness unless we make significant headway in cutting our federal budget deficit. However, to ensure that the budget deficit can be cut without precipitating a recession, we are going to need export-led growth to offset the contractionary effects of reduced government spending. That will require our major trading partners to reorient their economic policies to stimulate domestic demand and rely less on exports for growth.

Budget deficit reduction without export-led growth could send the U.S. and world economy into a serious downturn. Since growth has been driven, in large measure, by fiscal expenditures, any significant contraction there would need to be offset in order to maintain a healthy economy. Clearly, the last thing we can afford is a global recession. If our trade problems and the debt-servicing difficulties of our farmers, corporations, and developing countries look daunting now, these conditions clearly will be exacerbated in a recessionary environment.

To achieve sustained economic growth while reducing imbalances in the global economy will require substantial cooperation and coordination among the major industrial countries. Thus far, the necessary cooperation has been lacking as governments have pursued short-term national agendas at the expense of longer-term international goals. The institutional mechanisms exist to facilitate international coordination of macroeconomic policies. What has been missing is the political will. This must change if the United States and our major trading partners are to reduce global imbalances, avert protectionism, and maintain adequate levels of world economic growth.

Second, we must resolve the developing country debt crisis if our trade deficit is to be reduced. To "pay our way," we need robust and sustained growth in the developing as well as the rest of the world. Latin America in the 1970s was a growing market for U.S. exports. We need to stimulate that market, as a consumer of goods and services provided by U.S. suppliers.

Between 1980 and 1986, the U.S. manufacturers' trade surplus with Latin America dropped by $17 billion, from a surplus of $21.4 billion to $4.7 billion. Over half of this shrinking trade balance was due to a fall in U.S. exports to the region. This is a direct result of the policy responses of Latin governments to the debt crisis. Since external financing came to a halt, countries had to reduce imports sharply and increase exports to earn sufficient foreign exchange to maintain interest payments on the debt.

Moreover, adjustment policies imposed to deal with the debt problem may be reducing Latin America's future economic growth potential, as well as limiting the market for U.S. goods. Between 1983 and 1985 investment as a percentage of GDP fell by one-fourth compared with the previous five years.

Balancing competing interests to assure an equitable and successful resolution of the LDC debt crisis is extremely complex and difficult. What does seem clear, however, is that current policies are not achieving desired results.

A third basic problem exists in the fact that the rest of the world has essentially caught up with, and in some areas surpassed, the United States in technology. Remarkable advances have been made in the past 10 years that exceed the progress of the previous 50 years. The pace of change, the dissemination of information, know-how, etc., is phenomenal today. Clearly, there is no room for American industry to be complacent.

We must be prepared to face this reality head-on. Complaining about the way other countries do business will not solve our problems. We cannot remake the world in our image and force governments to pursue policies compatible with ours. The enormous task before us is to devise policies which maximize *our* ability to compete in this new world, not policies that isolate or insulate us from it.

Both government and the private sector have very important roles to play in dealing with this critical problem. One role of government must be to take steps to shore-up the multilateral trading system. In a world where the U.S. is no longer pre-eminent, it is very important to revitalize this system. Twenty years ago we could write the rules for the global economy, and we could walk away from them when they were not in our interest. No longer. Today, more than ever, we need a system of multilateral checks and balances if U.S. trade interests are to be preserved.

Our best hope—perhaps our only hope—to get beyond the current trade impasse is through negotiated agreements with our trading partners. We need existing rules strengthened and we need expanded coverage for services, investment, subsidies, and intellectual property. These are today's and tomorrow's trade problems.

Second, the United States must avoid protectionist solutions. It is very easy to raise barriers to imports. However, it is hard to see how restricting our markets will increase the competitiveness of U.S. industry. A tariff on imports can only harm U.S. exports. Managing trade in one sector inevitably will reduce competitiveness in another, because restricted trade raises prices and higher prices hurt users and, ultimately, producers.

Third, the U.S. government has an important role to play in helping to enhance the competitiveness of U.S. industry. Government research and development efforts should have commercial as well as defense applications where possible. Further, the federal government should cooperate with the academic and corporate communities in funding joint research efforts.

Government at the federal, state, and local levels must also support a first-rate system of education in this country. Without a well-trained, educated work force, American companies will be unable to develop and utilize the new technologies.

Finally, government needs to be sensitive to the competitiveness problems that excessive regulation can cause. Government at all levels must strike a careful balance such that U.S. industry is not excessively burdened compared with our foreign competitors while the environment and the health and safety of Americans are protected.

All that being said, however, I place primary responsibility for maintaining competitiveness squarely on the shoulders of American business. Certainly, for many corporations that had viewed their position in the U.S. and global markets as secure and somehow permanent, the last few years have been a rude awakening. A number of top American corporations have undergone substantial restructuring to maintain their fitness in an increasingly competitive global economy.

A NEW ORGANIZATION FOR GLOBAL COMPETITION

Eastman Kodak Company is no exception. It is safe to say that Kodak has undergone more changes in the last few years than in any other period of its first 100.

Peter Drucker, the internationally respected management philosopher, once noted, "Business has only two basic functions: marketing and innovation." Elaborating on that, any world-class corporation must have four priorities:

1. A significant, high-quality research effort.
2. A business unit structure that permits rapid transformation of the fruits of research into commercially viable, quality products.
3. A worldwide strategy of investment, production, and marketing.
4. The ability to monitor and improve both quality and cost.

In large measure, these priorities have been the keys to success throughout Kodak's history. But it also became clear several years ago that they needed updating and improvement to keep the company fit to meet the challenges of the global economy, an economy greatly different and offering vastly increased business challenges than just a decade before. Specifically, Kodak needed to modify the way it managed the *process* of innovation relative to the demands of marketplace.

Our recent priority has been to make the transition from idea—through development, through manufacturing—to the marketplace, more efficient. We clearly were not doing that as well as we could for a number of reasons. Most important, we historically managed the entire process from the top of the company. As a result, we were not reviewing innovations and the opportunities they represented in the most efficient manner possible. Looking at the structure of the company, it seemed obvious that decision making had to be pushed down in the organization. That was what led to reorganizing the company into our current business unit structure.

The most important objective underlying this reorganization was to ensure that business strategies and plans would be made at the right level for each business. In competitive global markets, a company like Kodak cannot afford an organizational structure that concentrates most decision making at the top. We are simply too large and too diverse. In reorganizing, we sought to have decisions made at the level of line responsbility. This has been very successful, and we are now accruing the benefits accordingly.

Eastman Kodak Company's new organizational structure has evolved to the point where today we have five major business groups in lieu of the previous two. Each one—Photographic Products, Commercial and Information Systems, Diversified Technologies, Eastman Chemicals Division, and Life Sciences Group—has all the resources necessary to achieve its goals. Although starting at different points, each has approximately the same potential for success, and each is held strictly accountable for its performance. Below this group level, we have a series of business units focused on specific customers in the marketplace. They are run by managers who have worldwide responsibility for their research, products, manufacture and marketing.

A second major step was taken in 1986 when we realigned our worldwide research and development activities. Our purpose was to link technology strategies more directly to business strategies. This realignment allows a corporate laboratory to concentrate on exploratory research to support future corporate directions. The other research laboratories are directed by our operating groups and business units.

All of this is aimed at matching technology with marketing objective and then driving that technology, more efficiently and cost-effectively, from concept through development to manufacturing. The result: innovative products conceived and commercialized in less time than ever before.

Finally, we created an Office of the Chief Executive to better allocate and focus top management's attention on activities of importance to the company. The OCE has three members: the Chairman and CEO, the President, and the Vice Chairman. This new structure has helped to buttress Kodak's sharper focus on business units.

PRODUCT DEVELOPMENT FOR A WORLD MARKETPLACE

It is probably accurate to say that, for years, Kodak was conservative in bringing new products to market. Traditionally, we wanted a product to be totally perfected before we would introduce it. In reaching that state, we relied almost exclusively on our own resources.

That strategy was appropriate and worked well in its time. But times have changed. The obvious problem is that you can lose a lot of ground to your competition that way. Customers can hardly be expected to wait for a propriety technology to be applied to new products.

For example, Ultra Technologies is the business unit that manufactures and markets the new lithium 9-volt battery, and also markets a full line of alkaline batteries. At the "old Kodak" typical development time for this kind of project would have been five to seven years. With Ultra Technologies, we did it in a little more than two. In February of 1984, parallel efforts began on the chemistry and design of the new lithium battery. At the same time, we were developing specifications for the manufacturing equipment and beginning construction on the plant inside the shell of an existing building. We were in production before mid-1986. This is, of course, the first lithium battery for the consumer market, and it represents a radical new design concept. In addition, Kodak has exercized decisive technology leadership necessary to get this new product into the marketplace.

Among the many specific examples that could be given, this one illustrates something that is disappearing at Kodak, the bureaucratic mentality that shuns taking individual responsibility for decisions. That sort of thinking strangles the process of getting things done quickly, ultimately undermining corporate fitness. Today, managers at the business unit level are seizing the initiative and taking responsibility for their own business strategies.

The flip side of the Ultra Technologies story is founded in the Supralife alkaline batteries. These are manufactured to Kodak specifications by a company in Japan. We could have done that in Rochester, but alkaline technology has been around since the 1930s. So we decided that we could demonstrate more technology and market leadership by concentrating on our proprietary lithium battery. The alkaline batteries are important in terms of completing our product offering in this field, but Kodak's resources would not have been well spent if we had diverted some of them to reinventing existing technology. We have not only injected this "entrepreneurial spirit" in our new lines of business like Ultra Technologies, we have also streamlined the process for our traditional lines as well. The results have been dramatic. For example, in 1986 we introduced 56 new photographic products, more than in any single year in the company's history.

We also are working to streamline the total flow of material within the company and reduce our product portfolio. Based on a study we made, 20 percent of our products contribute more than 90 percent of our revenue. That is changing.

For example, of more than 200 named products in our Graphics Imaging Systems Division, we identified more than 25 percent as targets for elimination. These represent older products with declining sales. Half of that consolidation effort was accomplished in 1986. In the process, we converted our customers to current technology better suited to meet their needs.

Similar product line evaluations are being conducted

throughout our business group. Thus, today we are both able to drop uneconomical products as well as develop new ones and enter new markets at a record pace. This is attributable in large measure to our new organizational structure.

A GLOBAL MANUFACTURING STRATEGY

In recent years, a significant portion of our capital spending has been targeted to improve quality and simultaneously enhance productivity.

One major program involves the design and installation of state-of-the-art equipment and process technology to achieve invariant high quality in photographic film and paper emulsion. Kodak is investing millions of dollars in this program with the goal of getting as close as possible to the theoretical limits of uniformity in performance as viewed by our customers. In addition, this capital project will provide us with worldwide product consistency without the local fine-tuning and adjustments that have traditionally been part of the process from plant to plant and from country to country.

This approach also involves a major investment in training to insure that the equipment can be operated identically at all of our sensitized goods plants around the world. In other words, operators will be charting and comparing the same process variables on a worldwide basis. This global approach will also enhance the technical transfer of new formulas between and among plants. The result will be reduced time required to put new formulas into production, which, in turn, means faster market entry with new or improved products.

This is very important for Kodak's "fitness" as we look to the future. The orthodox or traditional manufacturing strategy of concentrating on a few high-volume products is not adequate for fast-changing global markets. Our reorganization into lines of business has already modified that strategy. Within the next five years a broad range of products will provide the company with profits.

MANAGING A GLOBAL CONCERN

Management's job is really one of long-term planning. It is to make sure that there is a continuum of products coming along with sufficient funds allocated to them today to ensure their profitability tomorrow. A corporation must be managed in a pragmatic way. This means that if you are a worldwide supplier, you need to look at landed cost in each of your market areas: the cost of producing, shipping, duties...in other words, all of the costs associated with getting a product into a country.

Over time, that process will inevitably drive companies to supply from low labor-cost areas. The dimension that management has to add to that is the judgment of other factors, such as vested interests in existing plant locations. There are more human and monetary costs associated with abandoning existing capacity.

Indeed, for American companies to remain competitive in the world economy, management must think globally in terms of all aspects of the business, from markets, to production, to competition. Rethinking one's approach to doing business, and restructuring accordingly, is never easy. What makes it doubly difficult is that American corporations do not have the luxury of time. Competition is fierce and increasing daily. Clearly, American corporations have their work cut out. I believe they are up to the challenge.

Eastman Kodak Company has taken enormous steps to maintain its competitive edge. We believe that we are meeting the challenge, but there is no room for complacency in today's highly competitive world marketplace.

Anders Lindström

Anders Lindström, president and chief executive officer of the Carnegie Group, became his company's principal officer in 1986.

From 1983 to 1986, Mr. Lindström was president and chief executive officer of Bahco Group, a diversified Swedish engineering concern. Prior to his direction of Bahco, he was managing director of SELGA, a large electrical equipment wholesaler.

Mr. Lindström studied at the University of Uppsala and has over the course of his business career worked in banking, advertising, and management consulting.

He is a member of the boards of directors of Carnegie, Volvo Penta, the Swedish Power Administration, and many Carnegie Group subsidiaries.

In addition to other honors and responsibilities, Mr. Lindström was named Sweden's Manager of the Year for 1985.

9
NEW DIRECTIONS IN SWEDISH MANAGEMENT

Anders Lindström
Managing Director and Chief Executive Officer
The Carnegie Group, Sweden

Since its emergence as an industrialized nation a little more than a century ago, Sweden, whose population is still smaller than that of many large metropolitan areas, has developed a remarkably large number of enterprises that have established themselves securely in world markets.

At least a dozen Swedish companies are world leaders in their fields or in significant niches of important markets. The well-known names include: Electrolux (white goods), Volvo and Saab-Scania (cars, trucks, and aerospace), Ericsson (telecommunications), Atlas Copco (mining technology and industrial equipment), SKF (bearings), ASEA (power equipment and robotics), Hasselblad (cameras), Svenska Cellulosa (forest products), Alfa-Laval (separation equipment), AGA (industrial gases), and Esselte (office supplies). Scandinavian Airlines, owned by a consortium of national interests in three countries, but traditionally managed from headquarters in Sweden, also qualifies for this list. Other smaller companies, while hardly household names outside Sweden, have demonstrated their capacity to compete internationally.

Despite the proven ability of Swedes to manage companies with a high degree of success, their management styles—and the changes that have occurred in these styles during the past generation—have been largely neglected outside Sweden.

What might be termed the "original" Swedish management style was the product of a society that was late in exploiting the industrial revolution. It was essentially an authoritarian style, rooted in the traditions of the forestry and mining industries, in which self-contained complexes of forests, mills, forges, and farms—so-called *bruks*—were managed centrally and autocratically. Management was largely by fiat, with little concern for the finesses of motivation or other aspects of modern "employee relations" programs. Even at lower levels of the new industrial hierarchies, social distinctions were carefully preserved.

The changes in management style that have occurred during the past half-century may be attributed to a number of forces:

1. The existence of a demanding but well-disciplined labor movement whose political arm, the Social Democratic Party, has been an effective instrument for gaining increased participation in the industrial process.
2. Sweden's dependence on exports to maintain the high standard of living mandated by the welfare society. This has made it necessary for Swedish management to search out, evaluate, and implement all managerial techniques that may help industry remain competitive in the world market.
3. Increasing concern throughout the world for education, human welfare, and the individual's right to be informed of matters affecting his or her work life. Swedes have been among the leaders in transforming this concern into social activism.

In his recent book, *Scandinavian Management—Riding the Tide*, a survey of more than 100 companies in Denmark, Norway, and Sweden, the Norwegian consultant Eddie R. Sjöberg noted that the managements of these companies have looked primarily to American and Japanese industrialists and theorists for guidance. He also makes it clear, however, that the Swedes, in particular, feel that there is something distinctive about their own "corporate culture"—or "cultures"—that makes them cautious about full-hearted acceptance of foreign management styles. Sjöberg quotes Berth Jönsson, Vice President-Human Resources at Volvo, who concedes that Swedish management has been influenced by American theories and philosophies. But Jönsson, a long-time student of American and Japanese management styles, also observes:

> You soon discover cultural differences, and what can realistically be transferred. In this respect, Sweden may be considered a culture that lies between the Japanese collectivist culture and the American [which is] individualistically oriented. Naturally, we can import management, but under the distinct condition that we are able to adapt it to the characteristics of the individual work environments.

Interestingly, one of Sjöberg's findings documents a rather general belief that Swedes have a distinctive management style. Fewer than half (43 percent) of the Swedish respondents said they thought that Pehr G. Gyllenhammer of Volvo and Jan Carlzon of SAS, two top managers widely regarded as being close to the American pattern, were typical of what they associated with the Scandinavian management style.

Despite this reservation, we Swedes have not hesitated to borrow and buy American know-how in the management field. At one time or another most of the large Swedish multinationals seem to have retained American consultants to assist in analyzing, restructuring, and otherwise strengthening their operations. The works of Frederick W. Taylor, Peter Drucker, and Peters and Waterman are probably quoted as often in Stockholm and Gothenburg as in New York, Detroit or Schenectady.

Whether or not Swedish management style has developed independently or has been shaped by outside experience and theory is a matter for academicians to decide. More to the point, there have been perceptible changes in Swedish management style during the past generation. In my view, they may be summarized as follows:

1. A pattern of joint consultation with unions has been established.

2. We have become increasingly sensitive to factors that contribute to employee motivation.
3. We are placing increased emphasis on decentralization in virtually all areas except strategic planning and financial control.
4. We are becoming more receptive to the idea of genuine partnerships with non-Swedish companies.
5. And we are using information and communications techniques to a greater degree as management tools.

This is not to imply that Swedish management has lost all of its authoritarian features. Gyllehammar at Volvo, Carlzon at SAS, Hans Werthén at Electrolux, and Percy Barnevik at ASEA Brown Boveri—to name a few of our most successful managers—certainly are strong, decisive managers who combine charisma and personal authority. Others who are perhaps less well known outside Sweden—including Bo Berggren of STORA and Marcus Storch of AGA—are equally committed to the enlightened exercise of ultimate authority.

The unique Swedish management-labor partnership gives employee organizations statutory rights to participate in much decision making formerly reserved exclusively to boards of directors and CEOs. But our successful managers are able to work within these restraints. In fact, the strongest leaders initiated close cooperation with employees and their representatives long before "codetermination" procedures were regulated by law. This aggressive, pragmatic approach might well be characterized as "typically Swedish."

But willingness to accept advice and counsel, to participate in consultative bodies, and to build a consensus for policy and action should not be confused with the primary role and responsibility of a manager. He or she has to make the ultimate decisions and be prepared to stand by them.

THE CONCERN FOR MOTIVATION

Eighty-six percent of the Swedish managers who participated in Eddie Sjöberg's survey said they believed that the development of productivity within their companies was affected to a high degree by the motivation of their employees. We have found no easy solutions to this problem. But significant steps have been taken in recent years and there is evidence that employees are responding.

Swedish management has adopted two main approaches. One is based on the theory that the more the employees know about a company's objectives, strategies and operations, the more likely they are to share management's concerns and goals. Our managements have traditionally been required by law to keep employees informed about sales, earnings, and other aspects of corporate operations. Recently, more time and effort have been devoted to defining and clarifying corporate policy and demonstrating the employees' stake in the corporate process. Volvo, for example, has developed a comprehensive "Dialog" program in which a concerted effort is being made to increase employee awareness of the company's performance, objectives, and its role in the market place.

A second approach appeals more directly to the financial interests of employees. It consists of offering a company's Swedish employees—and, where feasible, employees of subsidiaries outside Sweden—opportunities to participate in their companies' growth by subscribing for debentures convertible to the companies' shares. Low-cost loans, which are used to finance the purchase of the convertibles have been offered by a number of companies. While this is no longer permitted, other forms of easy financing usually can be arranged. All employees are guaranteed the right to buy a minimum number of convertibles, but senior and middle managers are generally permitted to buy more than factory or office workers.

A number of companies have bonus systems of various types. Volvo was one of the first to introduce a plan covering all employees of its Swedish companies. The plan gives these employees the opportunity to participate in a "profit-related" bonus fund. Volvo's contributions to the fund are keyed to the company's return on capital employed.

In only a few cases have Swedish managers introduced rewards based on direct personal performance, such as those offered to successful sales personnel in the U.S. This type of motivation has not yet become part of the Swedish culture.

In addition to the specific programs cited above, I sense a genuine attempt to "humanize" relations with employees, to understand their on-the-job attitudes and desires, and to develop a working relationship based on cooperation rather than confrontation. While the rigid patterns and procedures for management-labor relations prescribed by law are still strong, they are being softened—one might say circumscribed—in subtle ways designed to gain acceptance for a company's long-term objectives.

INCREASED EMPHASIS ON DECENTRALIZATION

As Swedish companies have become larger, with more diversified product lines and expanded international operations, it has proved increasingly difficult to make all basic decisions in a single central location. As a result, the trend toward decentralized decision making has accelerated. More and more decisions involving operations, marketing, and allocations of budgets within sectors of the business have been delegated to "Business Area" units or divisions that are essentially product-oriented. This has had the effect of establishing more clearly defined profit centers. In some cases, it has also increased the possibility of greater synergistic effects in marketing-related product lines, or cultivating customers for a variety of a company's products. It has also eliminated the embarrassing situations in which more than one unit within a group compete for the same contract, sometimes offering notably different terms.

Decentralization has also meant reducing the number of staff workers at headquarters and delegating many staff functions to line companies. The staff functions that have been retained have in some cases been set up as independent profit centers, charging other company units for their services and, in extreme instances, seeking business outside the group to which they belong.

In theory, at least, the process of decentralization has simplified group structures, freeing top management to concentrate on long-term objectives, planning, and strategies.

Financial controls have also been retained firmly in the hands of senior management at group headquarters.

THE SEARCH FOR COMPATIBLE FOREIGN PARTNERS

We Swedes have, with some justice, been proud of the technologies our companies have developed and refined over the years. We have shared this know-how, to an extent, through licensing arrangements and ventures with companies in other industrialized countries. But few Swedish managers—or their boards of directors—have been willing to make commitments to full-scale partnerships in the international sphere. Nor has there been any compelling reason to do so until recently. Our technology has generally been state-of-the-art. Development costs, while high, have been controllable. Swedish workers enjoyed a deserved reputation for skill and craftsmanship. And large numbers of customers have been willing to pay a premium for quality products.

The high cost of technical development programs and the increasingly severe competitive conditions in world markets for capital goods are eroding the confidence that our high-tech companies can continue to "go it alone." The most striking development in this area has been ASEA's recent decision to form a partnership with Brown Boveri, the Swiss giant, establishing what will be the world's largest electrical and power equipment group. The change in attitude at Ericsson, the telecommunications manufacturer, has been less dramatic but no less significant. The company is already well established as the developer and successful marketer of one of the world's most successful telephone switching systems, and has preserved its independence zealously. Now, the company is welcoming international partners to share the exceptionally high development costs that it foresees in its industry. Important agreements have been signed with Digital Equipment, Texas Instruments, and IBM in recent years, and the company has indicated that others may be expected.

ASEA and Ericsson have assured their employees and shareholders that the integrity of their own operations will not be impaired. The fact remains that both companies have taken steps that portend a new direction in Swedish management style.

INFORMATION—THE NEW MANAGEMENT TOOL

The trend toward a new management style has become particularly apparent in the field of information. Although we are not the most secretive among multinational managers, we Swedes have not always been convinced of the necessity for disclosing details of our operations. Until about 20 years ago, for example, most of our companies issued a single interim report during the course of the year. This usually covered the period ending August 30 and did not reach the financial community until some time in October, about ten weeks before the end of the year.

The information provided to employees via company publications and so-called Work Councils—whose meetings attracted varying degrees of interest—seldom dealt in a substantive manner with the companies' objectives, plans, and strategies. Swedish management dutifully kept the unions informed, as required by law, but how much of the information filtered through to the factory floor or office desk was questionable.

It seems to me that this situation has altered drastically. Almost without exception, Swedish companies are now devoting substantial resources to surveys of employee attitudes, the publication of informative newspapers and magazines, and the prompt issuance of pertinent news. "Openness" and "candor" are more than abstract concepts in many corporate information guidelines, and I am convinced there is a generally sincere desire to honor them.

The demands of the international financial community have been one of the catalysts responsible for the new attitude toward information. As our companies increasingly sought to raise funds outside Sweden, they have discovered that analysts in New York and London, not to mention foreign regulatory authorities, were not satisfied with vague or incomplete answers to unexpectedly sharp questions rarely voiced in the Swedish market. Following some painful experiences, many of our managements are becoming adept at providing foreign investors with information that would have been closely guarded not too many years ago. "Road show" is a term now well rooted in the Swedish manager's lexicon. Swedish annual reports are also improving. Once regarded as difficult to interpret (due in part to the Swedish system permitting allocations of portions of profits to various reserves), these reports are now regarded as among the best-produced in the international community. A number of companies have been cited repeatedly for the quality of their financial reporting.

Full disclosure in one sector inevitably requires similar disclosure to other audiences. As a result, I think that Swedish employees, shareholders, and the general public now have access to information that is generally of high quality.

One of the interesting aspects of the trend toward decentralization has been that we have rediscovered the urgent need to communicate fully and efficiently with middle managers. We are relearning the importance of keeping them informed on corporate policy and practice as well as sales and earnings.

I see Swedish management moving toward a new style that has softened the edges of the old authoritarianism. Based on my own experience, this makes good sense in terms of human relations. And it serves the long-term interests of the companies we are paid to manage. In evidence, let me cite a specific case, the "rehabilitation" of the Bahco Group, in which I was recently privileged to participate.

THE BAHCO STORY

At year-end 1982, the Bahco, a medium-size Swedish engineering products group, was on the brink of bankruptcy. Due to a combination of factors, including earlier untimely international expansion, the company had been floundering for several years. In 1982, it reported an operating loss, before appropriations and taxes, of SEK 196 million on sales of SEK 2,596 million, with prospects of even greater losses in the year ahead. An analysis of the company by McKinsey & Company had not been encouraging. But early in 1983, the principal shareholders were determined to make a final effort to salvage the company. They had noted my experience with another troubled company, and they invited me to take over as managing director and chief executive officer.

In 1983, Bahco was a loosely structured organization of about 50 engineering companies with little in common save their reputations for quality products and an emphasis on production rather than marketing. The Group consisted of the following main units:

HIAB-FOCO   A world leader with 35 percent of the market for vehicle cranes. Manufacturing in Sweden, France, and Spain.
HYDRAUTO   Valves and other hydraulic equipment.
KRACHT   (West Germany) Hydraulics.
MECMAN   Pneumatics and electronics for industrial applications. Five plants in Sweden.
TOOL GROUP   Hand and power tools. Manufacturing in Sweden, U.K., France, and Argentina.
VENTILATION Air handling systems. Manufacturing in Sweden and France.

The company's best-known product was the Tool Group's line of adjustable wrenches, which had been invented by one of the company's founders nearly a century earlier. The largest unit, Hiab-Foco, a leading manufacturer of vehicle cranes, with a 35-percent share of the world market, was responsible for more than half of Bahco's losses in 1982. Only the Ventilation group, the second largest in its field in Sweden, had returned a small profit in that year. The challenge facing the new management was a formidable one.

STREAMLINING GROUP MANAGEMENT

From the beginning, I tried to indicate, through the size and make-up of the new Group management team, that we were going to have a lean, no frills operation. Our senior Group Management team consisted of only two other executives. I brought in Ralph Hammar, who had established a solid reputation at the Pharmacia Group, where he had been one of the principal architects of that company's internationalization, to serve as senior executive vice president—economy and finance. And I recruited Torsten Henriksson, who had designed and implemented successful information programs for ASEA and the Axel Johnson Group, to be our senior vice president—communications.

In a country where public relations and information experts had rarely been entrusted with responsibility at the policy-making level in industry, the selection of Henriksson was designed to send a signal. Communications would play a major role in the new management style at Bahco's headquarters, and the operating companies would be expected to strengthen their own internal and external communications programs. Equally important, the communications would be two-way.

While many strategies and tactics were involved in the turnaround of Bahco, this emphasis on communications was perhaps the most distinctive feature of the new management program. It served notice that we were going to have informal as well as formal communications with employees, shareholders, customers, and prospects. As suggested earlier, this represents a significant change in an industrial system in which authoritarian boards of directors and managers formerly conducted business with a minimum of formal communications.

KEY CONCEPTS IN THE BAHCO MANAGEMENT APPROACH

The management principles that our team sought to apply at Bahco were hardly novel. Many of them have been described in the literature on management theory and in case studies for many years. My basic contribution was to apply them—and persuade others to apply them—in a pragmatic way in a somewhat chaotic environment. Based on my earlier experience, I relied on five key principles:

Listen! Management Can Learn a Lot from Employees

In any organization the factory and office employees know more about their jobs, and how they can be performed more efficiently, than management ever can. Nearly all employees want to be part of a successful, respected organization; they have practical ideas and suggestions for improving profitability. It is up to management to listen, to create a climate in which employees can express themselves freely, without fear of ridicule, and with reasonable assurance that management is paying attention.

No less strongly, I believe in the benefits of "management by walking around." Shortly after I took over at Bahco, I made it a point to visit many of the company's plants in Sweden and other countries. Without making a ceremony of it, I wanted to be perceived as a visible symbol of the new beginning. I was careful at all times not to minimize the organization's difficulties, of which there were many. The employees and I both knew that the recovery program would involve painful changes in some sectors.

Simplify! Nearly Every Job Can Be Performed More Efficiently

This concept can be applied not only to the structure of the organization, and the need to eliminate unnecessary strata of supervision and management, but to the manner in which information was communicated as well. At Bahco, the simplification began at the top. The number of employees in our modest Group Headquarters in Stockholm was reduced to a bare minimum by eliminating some jobs and transferring other responsibilities to the operating companies. Those who remained received a clear message: cut paperwork and use simple direct language in all communications.

Restructure! Let's Not Be Afraid To Admit and Correct Mistakes

In our Swedish industrial lexicon, *rationalization* and restructuring often simply mean getting rid of dead wood and tightening up operations in a "crisis" situation when you have to eliminate jobs (adjusting production capacity to market requirements), dispose of unprofitable or incompatible units, and find partners to share the costs of certain operations.

We had to take all these hard steps at Bahco. The average number of employees within the Group declined from 8,400 in 1982 to 6,800 in 1984, the first full year under the new management. During the same period, we began negotiations to divest two of the Group's largest operating units—Bahco Record Tools in the United Kingdom and Hiab-Foco, the Swedish manufacturer of vehicle cranes. Both companies had been restructured successfully and were operating profitably. Virtually all product lines were also revitalized by scrapping outdated products, introducing new ones, and concentrating on select product-development work.

Restructuring at Bahco also meant decentralizing control over Group operations and delegating increased responsibility to managements in the operating companies. Goals and strategies were developed jointly but we wanted the local management teams to function largely without interference. Financial controls and decisions relating to the allocation of the Group's limited capital resources remained in the hands of the headquarters management team.

One of the most significant aspects of these changes, which affected all sectors of the Group, was the fact that they were implemented with a minimum of labor unrest. In a country where employee organizations are entitled by law to have a strong voice in nearly all management decisions, there was always a risk of confrontation when cost-cutting measures, no matter how obviously required, had to be taken.

Motivate! Most Employees Have
Untapped Potentials

There have traditionally been two primary factors motivating the performance of Swedish workers. One has been the well-merited national pride in Swedes' ability to turn out products and systems that have captured sizable shares of world markets. The other has been the expectation of a steadily rising standard of living based on collective wage and salary agreements, often enhanced by separate local contracts.

At Bahco, in the late spring of 1983, the effectiveness of these motivational factors was seriously hampered by morale problems. Two-thirds of the Group's sales were in markets outside Sweden, markets that had become extremely competitive. All divisions except Ventilation had reported losses in 1982. Thus the immediate prospects for anything more than minimum wage and salary increases were hardly attractive. Indeed, many employees had reason to feel that their jobs were in jeopardy.

The motivational approach we adopted at Bahco was based on seeking to persuade each employee that he or she could be an entrepreneur who could make a tangible contribution to a stronger, more profitable company, thereby assuring job security. We placed special emphasis on the need for more aggressive selling. Senior executives were encouraged to spend more time out in the field with customers and less time on administration. We challenged sales managers to abandon the old practice of cutting prices simply to maintain marginally profitable volume.

We also sponsored competition among the operating units, which was a relatively new promotional technique in Sweden, where it has generally been considered unbecoming to show up one's colleagues within the same corporate group. The Bahco contest, built around the theme "Sales Year 84" and conducted in three seasonal stages, was carefully crafted to provide a large number of winners and prizes. Companies were judged on the basis of their success in meeting certain established targets—order bookings, sales, operating income, etc.—and on their performance in more abstract areas: service attitudes, evidence of bold initiatives, creative selling, product development, and the like.

The basic objective of the competition, which was promoted heavily throughout the Group, was of course to focus attention on the importance of increased sales as a key to higher profitability. (A second competition the following year, "Ideas 85," promoted with the slogan "There Are No Ridiculous Ideas," produced a record number of suggestions for changing and improving the company's operations and products.)

Communicate! Let People Know Your Values and Expectations

From the start, the need for clear and frequent communication ranked among the most important concepts we had to implement. This involved more than merely communicating information. If our management team was to succeed in turning around the company, we had to communicate the tangible and intangible values we wanted to establish throughout the Group.

In her study of the transformation of Bahco, "Mutual Responsibility—The Path to Industrial Vitalization and Renewal," the Swedish management consultant and author Malle Jöever described our approach:

> The purpose in working on the basis of values was in part a rational one: it saved time in all communications. [It was also] partly emotional: it automatically created a sense of unity. The basic values and objectives judged to be important included the following:
>
> • Willingness and desire to communicate.
> • Openness and honesty.
> • Determination (to live up to the old, esteemed designation: "honest Swede").
> • Operations conducted in a manner that is good for society.
> • Creation of a sound business in which "people thrive and find satisfaction in their work, one in which they feel they are making a contribution through their job."

These values were not formulated unilaterally. They evolved from give-and-take discussions with managers and others throughout the Group. And they were based on realistic analyses of Bahco's corporate assets as well as its liabilities. We conceived them as *shared* values. And it soon became clear that managers who did not share them and who were not willing to communicate them down the line in their units would be free to pursue careers elsewhere.

THE FIRST CRITICAL MONTHS

Bahco's financial position was precarious when the new management took office in late May 1983. Additional capital was desperately needed to cover the costs of restructuring, rationalization, and much-needed product development. The immediate financial crisis was solved when the shareholders agreed to double the capitalization of the Parent Company, from SEK 90 m. to SEK 180 m., by subscribing for new shares. The Group's capital was further strengthened later in the year through the sale of a 40-percent interest in the Hiab-Foco subsidiary, which yielded SEK 54 m. We then had some breathing room in which to begin the difficult process of revitalizing the Bahco Group.

Many of the steps taken during this crucial period were the standard ones required in an organization whose survival was still very much in doubt. Managements of the operating companies had to be evaluated. Product lines had to be examined and culled, and decisions had to be taken on the allocation of funds for development projects. Objectives, strategies, and budgets had to be established, refined, and monitored. New financial control and reporting procedures had to be introduced and explained. Customers and prospects had to be reassured that the operating companies were in business to stay.

The distinctive feature of the new management style was the opening of new channels—channels of information and communication. Bahco had traditionally been a closed, compartmentalized organization, with little or no sense of group purpose. Generally speaking, the managements of the operating subsidiaries knew little or nothing about the problems, opportunities, or contributions of their sister companies. And the outside world was only vaguely aware that Bahco, once known as one of Sweden's prestigious small engineering companies, was now in serious trouble.

Later, in Bahco's annual report for 1983, I described the situation we had faced during the earlier period of restructuring. "A company is like a human being. When its misfortunes become overpowering, it loses self-confidence." We recognized that our primary task was to restore confidence at all levels of Group operations, to convince company managers, factory workers, and office employees that *they* could rebuild Bahco.

The information and communications program covered three categories of Bahco people. The first comprised about 40 managing directors, financial officers and information managers in the larger subsidiaries. The emphasis was on *continuing personal contact*, via telephone, office meetings, and less formal gatherings. Meetings with set agendas were scheduled at intervals of about eight weeks, each time at a different company's headquarters. One of the explicit objectives of these meetings, which have been described as miniature road shows, was to provide opportunities for the various management teams to present their companies, to get to know each other personally, and to share experiences of common interest. During this period, we also began to make plans for the first *international* conference of Bahco managers in the history of the company. This conference was held in the autumn of 1984.

The second audience category comprised a total of about 200 persons, including representatives of the unions. We communicated with this group primarily through a series of simple executive memos, covering a broad spectrum of information: the trend of business; advance reports; instructions, clarifications and suggestions; structural changes within the Group; managerial appointments, etc. The style was direct, informal and personal.

Our third audience consisted of *all* Bahco employees. Earlier managements had never attempted to communicate directly with all Group employees on a continuing basis. Again, the approach was simple, direct, and understandable. The medium was a series of "Talking Shop" brochures that were distributed in Swedish and English editions throughout the Group.

The first brochure was mailed to employees' homes only a few weeks after I took over as CEO. I knew the employees had doubts and hopes, fears and expectations. The name "Anders Lindström" meant little to them. They didn't want empty phrases or false promises. They wanted to know what kind of a person I was, what the values of the new management were, whether we could help them save Bahco—and their jobs.

The brochure contained what was probably the most candid message the average Bahco employee had ever received from top management. We did not conceal the gravity of the problems that Bahco faced, or the steps that might have been taken to solve those problems. I told the employees that failure to show initiative or take risks was a greater sin, in management's eyes, than making a mistake. I stressed the importance of simplifying operating procedures to make them more cost-effective. And I encouraged employees to believe that each of them, by performing even a small task more efficiently, could contribute to the security of their own jobs. It concluded with words that sum up my philosophy of dealing with other human beings in the management-labor partnership: "I need you." We followed up the first "Talking Shop" brochure with others dealing with specific subjects in down-to-earth language.

And, in all the conventional approaches to Bahco employees—company publications, reports to the union representatives, etc.—we tried to add an extra dimension to management information and communications programs in Sweden: a personal touch and a sense of genuine partnership.

Bahco had never had a Group-wide publication. Employees were scarcely aware of significant developments in companies other than their own. Torsten Henriksson, our information officer, moved quickly to correct this situation, establishing two informative publications—one in Swedish and the other in English. The subsidiaries in France, Germany, and Argentina received digest versions of the English periodical in their own languages.

At regular intervals, Henriksson also produced video cassettes containing interviews with senior executives, as well as features on various aspects of Group operations. For logistic reasons, distribution of these cassettes was limited to the Swedish companies.

We assigned a very high priority to producing an attractive annual report that would reflect the basic strengths of the Group and provide a clear picture of the progress being made to revitalize Bahco. The report—published in Swedish and English, with detailed digests in French, German, and Spanish—featured strong photographs of Bahco employees and a number of the Group's advanced products. There were a lot of positive things to say about Bahco's history, its people, and its products. We used this as the base for the confidence-building program.

For the first time in Bahco's history, copies of the report were distributed to *all* employees, as well as to the 2,000 shareholders, and to others in the financial community. To promote public confidence in the company, we offered copies to the general public through advertising in the Swedish business press. More than 2,000 requests were received, and the number increased in succeeding years.

Along with his other duties, Torsten Henriksson worked with the managements of the operating companies to strengthen the internal and external information functions in their units as well as at the Group level. He provided concise guidelines defining the broad-gauged capacities required of modern information managers, assisted in recruiting qualified personnel, and served as a consultant on specific problems. There could be no question in anyone's mind as to how we felt about the importance of information and communication.

WORKING WITH THE LABOR UNIONS

One of the potentially explosive situations facing the new management involved relations with the labor unions during a period when payrolls clearly had to be cut and divestments of certain operations were imminent. Swedish legislation covering "co-determination in the workplace" requires that the unions be consulted on virtually all matters affecting employees' jobs and welfare. Unions are also permitted to have their own consultants, who must be given complete access to a company's books. These regulations obviously can hamper a management's freedom of action and lead to protracted, time-consuming—and sometimes hostile—negotiations.

In this area, we were able to avoid serious problems through reliance on what was essentially a personal, informal approach. By adhering to a policy of early and full disclosure of all information affecting employees, we managed to gain understanding and acceptance for management moves that might otherwise have caused troublesome conflicts.

The confidence we gained was perhaps best illustrated by an unusual incident. When the consultant appointed by the union to protect the interests of the employees resigned to take another job, I offered to fill the vacancy, feeling that I understood their points of view and could be as helpful as any consultant brought in from outside. The union responded in a manner that was probably unprecedented in the history of Swedish management-labor relations. They accepted the offer. The only condition—which never had to be enforced—was that I had to agree to resign if the union was not satisfied with my services.

DISMANTLING THE SUPERSTRUCTURE

By the time the Bahco Group was integrated with companies of the Promotion Group early in 1986, it was not only profitable, but substantially stronger, structurally, than it had been when the new management took office. We had been successful in dismantling much of the "superstructure," whose acquisition half a decade earlier had encumbered the Group and caused its financial problems.

Hiab-Foco, the vehicle crane manufacturer, had been one of the more costly acquisitions, losing more than SEK 107 m. before appropriations and taxes in 1982 alone. This loss was reduced to less than SEK 2 m. in 1983, when a 40-percent interest in the company was sold to the Finnish Partek Group. The remaining interest was sold to Partek two years later.

Record Ridgway Tools, a well-established but only marginally profitable British company, had been acquired in 1980. By year-end 1984 it was apparent that the company, which had been operated under the name of Bahco Record Tools, would have better prospects under new ownership. The final agreement covering the sale of this unit to a consortium of the company's owners and outside investors was signed in March 1985.

Other structural changes during the 1983-1985 period included the divestment of a small company in the U.S., acquisition of the minority owners' interests in the Kracht companies in West Germany, and the purchase of two ventilation equipment companies, in Norway and in Finland.

As a result of these structural changes, Bahco's sales were reduced by approximately one-third. *But operating results had been improved from a loss of SEK 196 m. in 1982 to a profit, before appropriations and taxes, of SEK 164 m. in 1985.*

MEASURING ACHIEVEMENT AGAINST OBJECTIVES

In Bahco's final annual report, covering 1985 operations, we attempted to summarize what we had been able to do with the help of many, many people throughout the Group:

In 1983 we established a number of financial objectives for the Bahco Group:

* Return on assets should amount to 17 percent.
* We should have at least 10 percent of our assets in liquid funds.
* Our solidity should amount to at least 30 percent.
* Our profit margin (profit as a percentage of sales) should exceed 12 percent.

The record for 1985 shows the following:

* The return on assets was 15.5 percent. We came close to meeting our objective.
* Liquidity amounts to 18 percent of total assets. We achieved our objective.
* Our solidity at year-end was 25 percent. This indicates that we still have a bit to go.
* Our profit margin was equal to 12 percent of sales. We achieved our objective.

The steps we took to reach our objectives may be summarized in the following terms: concentration of operations, more direct paths to decision-making, "profiling" the individual businesses, more efficient use of capital and creation of a new information climate. We strengthened the managements of Bahco companies, we built up functioning organizations that can stand on their own two feet and take full responsibility for their operations. And, last but not least, we corrected our problems ourselves...A few years ago Bahco was a company without self-confidence, crushed by crises and losses. Out of this critical situation have emerged businesses that are infused with a sense of employee involvement, with strength and confidence in their own capacities.

Many persons—from the principal shareholders who provided additional funds in the darkest days to the clerks who used office supplies more economically—were entitled to share credit for the turnaround.

SUMMING UP

The significance of the Bahco turnaround lies not only in the techniques employed, but in the impact their successful application can have on the management styles of other Swedish companies.

The principles we applied—decentralized operations, clearly formulated communication, use of information as a management tool, employment of motivational devices, direct, informal personal contacts, etc.—were not novel. But by demonstrating that they could be used productively and in combination, we perhaps contributed to the evolution of a new style of management in Sweden.

We never lost sight of our two basically indivisible tasks: to provide a fair return for the men and women who had put their capital at risk in the company, and to assure the jobs of the greatest possible number of our employees. I think we also demonstrated that the management function can be "humanized" without loss of dignity, prestige—or profits.

John F. McGillicuddy

John F. McGillicuddy, chairman of the board and chief executive officer of Manufacturers Hanover Corporation and Manufacturers Hanover Trust Company, started his banking career with Manufacturers Hanover in 1958. He was elected senior vice president in 1966, and was advanced to executive vice president and assistant to the chairman in 1969. In 1971, he became president and in 1979, chairman of the board, president, and chief executive officer. In 1982, he relinquished the positions of president of Manufacturers Hanover Corporation and Manufacturers Hanover Trust Company.

Mr. McGillicuddy is a director of Allegis Corporation, the Continental Corporation, Kraft, Inc., and USX Corporation. He is chairman of the board of Manufacturers Hanover Limited, and is a member of the Business Roundtable, the Business Council, the Association of Reserve City Bankers, the Conference Board, Inc., and the Federal Advisory Council of the Federal Reserve System. He is a trustee of Princeton University, the New York Public Library, and a director of the National Football Foundation and Hall of Fame, Inc., the New York City Partnership, Inc., Economic Development Council of New York City, and the New York Chamber of Commerce and Industry.

Mr. McGillicuddy holds a law degree from Harvard Law School and a bachelor of arts degree from Princeton University. He holds honorary doctoral degrees from the College of New Rochelle, Grant College, St. John's University, St. Bonaventure University, Pace University, College of the Holy Cross, and St. Francis College.

10
THE
INTERNATIONALIZATION OF
FINANCIAL MARKETS

John F. McGillicuddy
Chairman and Chief Executive Officer
Manufacturers Hanover Corporation, USA

The ever accelerating pace of change is an often touted feature of contemporary economic affairs. The only thing constant is change, we remind ourselves, and this has given rise to another modern phenomenon—the tendency of concepts rapidly to assume shopworn status, often before the verity they proclaim has fully taken hold.

Global economic interdependence is one such theme. We talked about it routinely throughout the postwar era. So much so, in fact, that when Prime Minister Thatcher used the term in a 1979 speech to the Foreign Affairs Council, she felt obliged to "apologize for the jargon."

It was only as the 1980s unfolded, however, that the impact of global interconnectedness began to be felt in full with the almost total internationalization of credit and capital markets. This idea of a single global financial marketplace was also a notion that had grown dog-eared before fruition, the subject of countless speeches before the annual joint meetings of the World Bank and International Monetary Fund. But by the mid-1980s, theory had become stark reality. The world's financial markets were one.

It meant that both around the clock and around the world, market participants could now raise equity, borrow money, and make investments in the currency and rate maturity of their choosing. They could even suddenly change the character of their assets and liabilities by switching from one currency into another or from one maturity into another, or both simultaneously. Corporate treasurers and their bankers could now scan the world in search of the best interest rates, the best currency deals, the best maturities and rate structures, as well as the best environment for their debt and equity offerings.

This development may have been evolutionary, but the result was clearly revolutionary. It created the ability to access money anywhere in the world in much the same way that industrial firms source parts and raw material from outside their home manufacturing bases. Just as an American-made car might contain tires from Korea, upholstery from Hong Kong, engine parts from Japan, a financial instrument issued on behalf of an American company might draw in funds from investors on five continents.

Multinational participation was not necessarily new. Syndicated credits involving banks from around the world had been around for decades. What was new was the ability to bypass banks as an intermediary and appeal directly to the transnational investor. More and more, as we shall see, the role of banks in serving their large multinational customers— corporations, financial institutions, and government agencies—would switch from being *providers* of credit to being *arrangers* of credit.

Former Controller of the Currency, John Heinmann, described the internationalization of financial markets as "one of the few conspicuous successes in international structure during the postwar period." J.P. Morgan & Co., in its 1986 annual report to shareholders, suggested that "the integration of the world's capital markets is perhaps the most profound economic development of this decade. Not only do these markets finance trade and investment; they now also permit a more efficient use of capital throughout the world economy." Our financial markets had not just changed in degree; they changed in kind.

UPROOTING CONVENTIONAL WISDOM

The globalization of credit and capital markets is a salutory development, but one not without its dislocations. For one, it has assured that almost everything that happens in our world can have an impact on everything else—and frequently *does*, often in defiance of traditional laws of economics.

For example, most of us were brought up believing that trade imbalances were self-correcting—that is, a country's worsening trade deficit would soon result in a weakened currency. So much for received wisdom. In today's interwoven world, it is capital flows, not trade flows, that often determine the value of a currency.

Consider the somewhat perverse cycle of events that has characterized much of the current decade: A growing U.S. budget deficit leads to higher real U.S. interest rates as the markets demand a new inflation premium. Higher rates, in turn, attract foreign investors to U.S. government securities. This flow of funds, in turn, drives up the value of the dollar. An overvalued dollar makes our exports uncompetitive and imports to us a bargain. Increased sales to the U.S., then, give our trading partners all the more wherewithal to go on buying our paper and financing our debt.

The internationalization of credit and capital markets had turned conventional wisdom on its head. Self-correcting currencies is one example. Another attends what had been dogma with respect to the factors leading to a credit crunch.

Economics theorists used to warn, with empirical wisdom to back them up, that a growing appetite for debt on the part of the government would soon lead to a classic credit crunch—the crowding out of private-sector borrowers in favor of the most credit-worthy borrower of all, the U.S. Treasury.

Given globalization, however—along with the massive financial imbalances that had built up around the world—Washington no longer needed to be concerned with crowding out domestic borrowers. The government could, and *did*, get all the funds it needed overseas. So much so, in fact, that in 1984, the U.S. Treasury paid out more in interest to foreign holders of government debt than the Federal government would spend on foreign aid that year.

By 1986, foreign purchases of Treasury securities were accounting for nearly one-quarter of such sales, up from only 4 percent as recently as 1983. At one point in the summer of 1986, Japanese purchasers alone took an estimated $4 billion of a $9 billion Treasury-bond offering, according to a report in the *Wall Street Journal*.

But while a credit crunch didn't develop, another kind of crunch did. Call it a crowding out of American labor and a crowding out of America's true productive capacity.

America's budget and its ripple effect throughout global financial markets had saddled American manufacturers with an artificial disadvantage on world markets. By 1983, an overvalued dollar was in effect taxing our exports by 25 percent and subsidizing imports by a like amount. The result was the largest trade gap in our nation's history—a condition that has since begun to reverse itself, but only modestly to date. Events have been so fast-paced that, in only three years, the United States had gone from being the world's No. 1 creditor—a position built up over two-thirds of a century—to being its No. 1 debtor. At the end of 1986, Americans owed nearly $200 billion more than was owed them.

Globalization means that authorities in Washington—or in any capital, for that matter—can no longer map policy in disregard for what may be happening elsewhere. As one economist has observed, when the next U.S. recession comes, "for the first time ever it is likely to be caused by external factors."

In one of his last appearances before Congress prior to retiring as chairman of the Federal Reserve Board, Paul Volcker noted that "to make an intelligent forecast nowadays, one must first study economic prospects abroad. That's a new kind of world to be living in, but we are living in it." He also pointed to the stickiness of attempting to take international concerns into account when crafting domestic policy. "A world of more widely dispersed power may have some advantages, but ease of achieving consistent and coherent leadership is not among them," he observed. "Intellectually, it is easy to recognize our interdependence. But, in practice, the instinct is to exert our independence."

The conflict between what must be done at home and what must be done abroad is not easily resolved. Economist Marina von Whitman has described the dilemma as "the tension between economic interdependence and the demand for domestic autonomy on the part of nation-states; the trade-off between policies that would promote the achievement of specific national economic or political goals and those likely to promote the viability of a coherent international economic system."

Despite our new age of economic summitry, these conflicts still very much exist. Thirty-five years ago, Wendell Willkie suggested that "political internationalism without economic internationalism is a house built upon sand." Today, he might have reversed that statement. For it is the financial and economic interdependence of nations that has become a fact of life. We are more closely stitched together economically than we are politically.

Not that this fact is ignored. It wasn't so long ago that national leaders would have met in summit only to discuss the grand designs of armaments and alliance. Starting in 1976, the year of the first economic summit, heads of governments began meeting to address the recycling of petrodollars, disparities in economic growth rates, and inflation—even the regulation of foreign banks. These may not be the issues of high statecraft that historians write about. But they matter as much. Perhaps even more.

A FRENZY OF INNOVATION

Public policy issues aside, the internationalization of credit and capital markets brought with it a veritable frenzy of financial innovation, as evidenced by those CATS, TIGERs, STAGS, ZEBRAS and other zoological acronyms that soon began to graze the pages of the *Wall Street Journal* and the *Financial Times*. Each denotes a new form of financial instrument or some new variation thereof. STAGS, for example, is short for sterling transferable accruing government securities. ZEBRAS is short for zero-coupon euro-sterling bearer or registered accruing securities. All take advantage of, in one way or another, a marketplace that has become truly global in scope and singular in its capacity to meet a myriad of complex financial requirements.

In 1985 alone, some 20 new credit and capital market instruments were introduced. They roughly divided down into four main groupings—funding instruments, underwriting instruments, hedging instruments, and arbitraging instruments. Included were everything from zero-coupon bond convertibles to collateralized securities backed by automobile loans and computer leases.

The year also saw the emergence of non-dollar floating rate issues and non-dollar zero-coupon bonds and a continued explosion in the number of international bond issues and a concurrent decrease in syndicated bank credits—one result, as we shall see, of the *disintermediation* and *securitization* of the credit process.

The issuance of international bonds increased by 50 percent in 1985 versus 1984. Volume, measured in dollars, rose to nearly $100 billion, up from $80 billion in 1984 and $47 billion in 1983.

In 1986, the growth was even more staggering. Bond financing in the international markets grew to $225 billion. Tellingly, new international bond issues in 1986 were denominated in no less than 16 different currencies. Moreover, of 1986's total, some 70 percent were swap-driven—that is, they featured the manipulation of currencies, interest rates, or maturities to achieve the best deal for both issuer and investor.

Swaps became the most visible innovation. By 1986, the annual volume of interest rate and currency swaps had grown to more than $300 billion. My own institution was involved in roughly 10 percent of this market. We engineered nearly $30 billion in interest rate swaps, currency swaps and forward rate agreements. Included were several hybrids. But all aimed at reconciling what might be called the volatile world differences between users of funds on the one hand and providers of funds on the other.

Swaps, in essence, allow the three characteristics of a financial instrument—namely, rate, maturity, and currency of denomination—to be addressed separately. Bankers call it "unbundling." An example is an instrument that Manufacturers Hanover pioneered in 1985. By today's standards of financial complexity, it seems simplistic in comparison, but the example does illustrate both the use of swaps and the global meandering that can take place in seeking to address multiple requirements.

We underwrote the first collateralized mortgage obligation to be denominated in Swiss francs. The borrower was Glendale Savings and Loan, located in southern California. Glendale secured the issue with thousands of individual single-family mortgages it had made in its local market.

Those buying the instrument were private investors and institutional money managers sitting halfway around the world in Zurich and Geneva, many of whom, I suspect, had never even been to southern California, to say nothing of possessing an in-depth knowledge of the American housing market.

But the global aspects of the deal didn't end there. Glendale wasn't interested in funding itself in Swiss francs. The only reason we had taken it to the Swiss capital market was to achieve a lower rate. What Glendale really wanted was a fixed-rate U.S. dollar obligation. So we executed a fixed-rate dollar obligation.

That transaction resulted in an open Swiss franc position, for Glendale had agreed to remit Swiss francs. But, at this point, it didn't possess the francs required. So we searched for a counter party to a currency swap. But, in the meantime, we hedged our open Swiss franc position with foreign exchange dealers in New York and London.

This, in turn, left us with a fixed-rate obligation. The market for currency swaps, however, required a floating rate obligation. So we executed a dollar-rate swap with a number of American corporations and banks.

The search for a counter party to currency swap ended in Tokyo with a Japanese company that had a stream of Swiss francs coming in but wanted a dollar obligation.

Thus, what had started in southern California with a pool of residential mortgages ultimately led to a currency swap in Japan with several interest rate swaps in between. Glendale ended up with the lower cost, fixed-rate dollar obligation it was after. Investors in Zurich got a ten-year Swiss franc bond. An industrial firm in Japan got the opportunity to convert a stream of Swiss francs into a floating dollar obligation. And everybody was happy, including Manufacturers Hanover, which had stood in the middle of it all and received a handsome fee.

THE FORCES BEHIND INTERNATIONALIZATION

As noted, the internationalization of credit and capital markets was an evolutionary development. But it picked up impressive momentum in the early 1980s due to the confluence of three interconnected forces:

1. Rapid advancements in the application of information and computer technology.

Throughout the 1970s, major banks and other financial institutions had invested heavily to put in place their own global communications networks. In a sense, we had "wired" the world. The resulting ability to deliver reliable information on demand worldwide altered dramatically the way in which credit and investment was to flow between providers of funds on the one hand and users of funds on the other.

Efficient markets, the textbooks, say, can only exist when both potential parties to a transaction possess roughly the same degree of information. As we shall see, this is precisely what electronic technology made possible.

2. The highest real rates of interest since World War II, unprecedented volatility in the behavior of interest rates and currency rates, and equally unprecedented imbalances between the financial and economic performances of national economies.

Each brought about the need for new financial techniques as market participants sought to protect themselves against the unknown, often learning to benefit from volatility in the process. For example, foreign exchange transactions totaled $80 billion in 1986, but only $4 trillion of the trading was connected to the financing of trade. The rest was essentially currency speculation.

Market forces are useful to keep in mind. For financial innovation didn't just happen because someone decided to bring a better mouse trap to market. As we shall see, innovations in financial technique—including such non-credit activities as international cash management—were a direct response to the dramatic increase in the time value of money we began to witness in the late 70s, along with levels of volatility never before experienced.

3. Financial deregulation, including the breaking down of national barriers to money and capital flows and a gradual freeing up in terms of what services various types of financial institutions are permitted to offer.

Both were in response to naked market forces. Financial deregulation is often viewed as being the product of shifting national political predelictions; a move to the right, if you will—first in the U.K., then in Germany, the U.S., France, and elsewhere. But, in fact, as we shall see, recent financial deregulation has been more the result of practical economic imperatives that know no ideology.

Now let's look at each force behind internationalization in greater detail.

INFORMATION TECHNOLOGY

Bit by bit—or, more precisely, byte by byte—information technology began to step out of banking's back office in the 1970s and into the maelstrom of a financial services revolution.

Technology in banking used to be primarily a support activity. In the 1960s, it helped us attack the paper mountain through improved electronic processing techniques. This led in the early '70s to quantum gains in productivity in such activities as check processing and check reconcilement, and brought about the nascent stages of corporate cash management.

By the late 1970s, however, information technology was no longer merely supportive. It had become strategic, directly influencing almost everything a bank did.

As the 1980s progressed, modern banking, it might be said, was becoming a new information industry. According to bank stock analysts at Salomon Brothers, U.S. commercial banks in 1985 spent an estimated $8.2 billion on systems technology, defined as hardware, systems software, applications software, and systems-related telecommunications. That's more than was spent by any other industry, except for the telecommunications industry itself.

The 1985 figure was nearly two times the $4.2 billion that banks had invested in systems technology in 1981 and accounted for more than half of the banks' discretionary spending.

Technology's most readily apparent imprint, of course, has been on consumer banking. Indeed, technology is synonymous with financial services for the consumer, what with 24-hour cash machines, point of sales terminals, and banking at home via personal computer. But, in fact, technology's most dramatic influence has been on the services banks provide to corporations, governments, and other banks.

Twenty years ago, Marshall McLuhan had forecast the eventual arrival of a "global village," the result, he predicted, of electronic interdependence. By the mid-1980s, banks had constructed their own global village.

There came into being a new type of competitor—a dozen or so institutions that could define themselves as global electronic banks. These banks possess three things in common:

1. A broad, worldwide network of branches and subsidiaries, each with the ability to deal in local currencies and to process multiple transactions on site. In other words, the ability to function as an indigenous bank. In the case of Manufacturers Hanover, we have a full operating presence in 32 of the world's major financial centers, from Bahrain to Buenos Aires, from Manila to Madrid.

2. A Global communications network capable of linking overseas offices to one another to create a timely and reliable pool of global information. In our case, our own global communications network, which we call GEONET, connects not only our overseas locations, but our major domestic offices, as well, in New York, Los Angeles, Chicago, Miami, and Atlanta. GEONET—a proprietary internal data transmission network— utilizes a variety of components such as leased lines from RCA and AT&T, satellite links, and microwaves. The decision to

build the network was not based on the needs of any one product. We felt that a single standard network—one that we owned ourselves—was necessary to meet a variety of emerging global requirements while at the same time minimizing the cost of transmitting data.

3. The hardware and software capabilities to allow customers to access the bank's internal information systems on a real-time basis. TRANSEND is Manufacturers Hanover's trademark for a broad array of information and transaction-initiation services. They literally link us to our customer's office, and vice versa, using personal computers. One example is the customer's ability to initiate letters of credit by entering instructions in a PC. Forty percent of our letter-of-credit volume is now completely accomplished electronically, reducing costs and errors and speeding up turnaround time.

Facilitated by the advent of banking's global village, the globalization of financial markets has led to the existence of a huge pool of money moving freely around the world. Payment instructions now course around the globe, rushing along fiber-optic cables and bouncing off satellites at near the speed of sound. Currently, there is the capacity to transmit data at the rate of 152,300 characters per second, and that will probably seem like a crawl five or ten years from now.

What has been created, in effect, is a high-tech money pump which *each day* circulates in excess of $1 trillion, or about one-quarter of America's *annual* gross national product. Consider two conduits of these flows:

Clearinghouse Interbank Payments System. Based in New York City, *CHIPS*, as it is known, is jointly operated by 120 U.S. commercial banks. It specializes in funds transfers and financial messages resulting from international trade and foreign exchange transactions. CHIPS volume more than tripled since 1981. By 1988, it was processing more than 200,000 transactions a day.

Society for Worldwide Interbank Financial Telecommunication. A joint venture of hundreds of financial institutions all over the world, *SWIFT*, as it is called, is a transnational data processing and telecommunications system conveying financial transaction and instructions and other financial information between member banks. The volume of messages transmitted via SWIFT each year increased from 21 million in 1981, the year after the network went live, to more than 830 million in 1986.

As these two examples make clear, electronic technology has increased the velocity and volume of money flows. But it has also contributed to a change in the very nature of the credit process itself and has begun to alter the role of financial intermediaries. The trends brought about are now referred to as *disintermediation* and *securitization*.

Disintermediation is a term that used to refer only to the outflow of bank deposits—the movement of money out of banks and into alternative savings and investment instruments, such as what occurred earlier in the decade when household savings began to move out of banks and in money funds sponsored by brokerage firms. In today's context, disintermediation also refers to the fact that, more and more, money is flowing more directly from suppliers of funds to users of funds. Credit itself is being disintermediated. Traditional financial intermediaries such as commercial banks still stand in the middle of these flows. But instead of actually providing credit and creating an asset on our books, more and more we are structuring instruments—securities—that are then distributed widely into the international market.

An early example of disintermediation—and one from which U.S. commercial banks are still barred participation domestically—is the commercial paper market. Corporations, in effect, lend money directly to one another, bypassing the banking system altogether. Unlike a bank loan, commercial paper is a security, which brings up that other new term in today's financial lexicon—*securitization*, or the turning of non-marketable debt into marketable debt.

Through securitization, assets formerly held on a lender's books are packaged and converted into blocks of securities that the originating institution then sells to other investors—most typically, pension funds, insurance companies, and other banks.

As one journalist observed, "the financial services industry is attempting to securitize everything that moves." The facts bear him out. According to Salomon Brothers, asset-based security volume swelled to $270 billion in 1986. Much of the rise was spurred by an explosion in collateralized mortgage obligations, or CMOs, of the type we saw in the Glendale example. But there has also been a dramatic increase in the securitization of car loan receivables and credit card receivables.

Manufacturers Hanover helped to pioneer the later. In 1985, we brought to market the first revolving credit back-up facility using credit card receivables as collateral—this, a transaction for MBank in Dallas. Two years later, we arranged the first public note issue securitizing loans collateralized by insurance premiums—a $160 million transaction for Reliance Premium Credit Corporation. We led the issue. Correspondent banks in seven countries participated in the underwriting group.

In addition to packaging and selling loans already on their books, banks now often make major new loans with securitization in mind at the outset. An example is found in those megabuck loans we've seen in recent years in connection with leveraged buy-outs. At Manufacturers Hanover, our Acquisition Finance Group may commit $500 million to a deal, but end up keeping only a small portion of the credit. The balance is participated out to other banks and financial institutions throughout the country and throughout the world.

Reduced to their bare essentials, these trends we know as *disintermediation* and *securitization* simply mean that it is the markets themselves that are intermediating the flow of funds. Lending is channeled through the markets in the form of tradeable paper, or securities. But trading and market depth are what allow this to happen on a global basis. And trading and market depth are, in large part, the results of better communications and analysis. And that gets us back to information technology applied globally. Consider the law of economics mentioned earlier. Efficient markets exist when all parties to a transaction possess roughly the same degree of information. That has been the contribution of banking's global village.

The *Financial Times* of London presented a compelling way of getting at much the same point: "costs, competition and deregulation may be the driving force behind the financial services revolution. But its direction is now being determined by microelectronic technology."

VOLATILITY

The cover of Manufacturers Hanover's 1985 annual report provided a quick snapshot of the roiling sea that the world's financial markets had become.

A linear graph charted the behavior of four benchmark statistics since 1971—the trade-weighted dollar, the prime lending rate, the annual consumer price index, and the U.S. budget deficit. The four lines appear fairly tranquil as the period begins. By 1978, the lines begin to snake from top to bottom of the page, each with a life of its own. Enter what Peter Drucker has called, "The Age of Discontinuity." Or, perhaps more accurately, the title of Tom Peters' latest book, "Thriving on Chaos."

Superimposed on, in, and around the lines is a series of headlines summarizing major economic and financial events for each year. A brief review since 1977 is telling.

1977. Dollar hits all-time low. U.S. trade deficit tops $25 billion, highest ever. Western leaders meet in London for economic summit.

1978. Carter moves to support sagging dollar; steps up gold sales. Fed raises discount rate a full point to 9.5 percent. Prime rate ends year at 11.75 percent, four points higher than at start.

1979. Fed declares all-out war on inflation; raises discount rate to 12 percent and imposes new reserve requirements. Gold closes year at $506, up from $246 a year earlier.

1980. Prime rate changes 47 times; hits record 21.5 percent. Congress votes to phase out deposit rate ceilings. Credit restraint program is imposed. Gold breaks $800.

1981. World recession deepens. U.S. employment rate hits 10.8 percent. Business failures reach post-Depression high. Dollar rebounds sharply.

1982. Real rate of interest reaches 8 percent, a postwar high. Federal deficit swells to $111 billion. Debt ceiling raised to $1.4 trillion. Eurobond market tops $50 billion.

1983. Most deposit-rate ceilings removed in U.S. Bank money market accounts grow to $350 billion. U.S. loans at foreign banks reach $85 billion. U.S. deficit hits $195 billion.

1984. Commercial paper tops $225 billion. Eurobond volume reaches $227 billion. Foreign capital flows to U.S. exceed $100 for year. Average daily CHIPS volume breaks $350 billion.

1985. Group of Five nations agree to intervene in foreign exchange markets. Dollar hits historic high against most major currencies. U.S. reports largest ever trade deficit. The disintermediation of credit flows picks up pace.

As this quick scan makes clear, volatility and uncertainty had become characteristic of free markets. And this, along with high real rates of interest—that is, the spread between nominal interest rates and the rate of inflation—brought about the demand for uncharted new levels of financial innovation.

New financial techniques came in the form of those innovative funding, underwriting, hedging, and arbitraging instruments mentioned earlier. But innovation also came in the form of sophisticated cash management programs in response to a new eleventh commandment: Thou shalt not leave fallow a single drachma of idle cash.

With the real or effective cost of money surging to 8 percent, all financial services customers began to take this commandment to heart. But it was the corporate treasurer who turned it into an obsession. A rapid rise in the time value of money had greatly increased the opportunity cost of every unit of cash not optimally employed. It meant that every dollar must be present and accounted for.

Treasury workstations, developed by computer programmers at major banks, were introduced into the market. They employed both hardware and software to allow a corporate treasurer's office to analyze and then execute many different kinds of transactions at the same time, using upwards of ten video screens and keyboards simultaneously.

Perhaps if and when a greater degree of rate and currency stability returns to our markets, the demand for complex credit and non-credit services will abate. More likely, however, the frenzy of financial innovation will continue apace. For the genie of financial sophistication is out of the bottle. The toothpaste is out of the tube.

DEREGULATION

As noted, the forces behind the internationalization of credit and capital markets are closely intertwined. The current trend of financial deregulation obviously goes hand in hand with globalization and innovation. And deregulation has much to do with market volatility and high real rates of interest. But it is difficult at times to determine which came first.

Globalization and financial innovation are now clearly being helped by deregulation. But it was regulations themselves that had in part helped bring about globalization and innovation in the first place as market participants found ways to get around existing restrictions.

The Euromarket, for example, originally got started, in part, as a black market for U.S. dollars in the wake of America's interest-equalization tax of the 1960s. And our domestic commercial paper market, it could be argued, really developed as a response to the legislated inability of commercial banks to pay interest on corporate deposits of 30 days or less.

Moreover, by bumping up against preexisting regulatory barriers in national markets, the trends of globalization and innovation soon demanded a choice from governments—either loosen your restrictions or weaken your competitiveness in financial services, with a resulting loss of jobs, tax revenues, and prestige.

Even more to the point, the trends of globalization and financial innovation might not have developed at all were it not for such seminal, macroeconomic forces as high real rates of interest and unprecedented volatility.

Consider just one isolated case in the United States—the almost total lifting five years ago of interest-rate ceilings on consumer deposits. This turned retail banking on its head and unleashed a floodgate of new competition and new products. But it had virtually nothing to do with the free-market precepts of Reaganomics. Instead, it resulted from the fact that market rates of interest had soared to 20 percent at a time when banks were still limited to paying 5 percent on their deposits. The result was that brokerage-house money funds—which faced no rate restrictions—soon ballooned to $200 billion. This dangerous disintermediation of the banking system, I submit, would have called upon any politician of any political persuasion to act.

Market forces, not politics, was also the impetus behind London's "Big Bang." It is also what caused a socialist government in France to reopen the French Eurobond market and to abandon its Keynesian expansion several years ago in the face of hostile capital movements. As I see it, the *politics* of deregulation has become one and the same with the *economics* of deregulation, and will remain so.

In the United States, unfortunately, the final word on financial deregulation has yet to be written. Fifty-five years after the Glass-Steagall Act was rushed through Congress during FDR's first "100 days", commercial banks are still barred from doing domestically what they can do in most other financial markets—namely, deliver a full range of lending and underwriting services. Glass-Steagall, which separated commercial banking from investment banking, hardly made sense in 1933. It makes absolutely no sense in today's world of disintermediation and securitization.

In 1987, Senators William Proxmire and Jake Garn introduced a bill that would remove such artificial barriers and allow commercial banks to underwrite most forms of securities while giving commercial banking powers to investment banks. In introducing the measure, Senator Proxmire described Glass-Steagall as a "protectionist dinosaur—a fossil held over from a bygone era. The American economy and the American people deserve better."

Federal Reserve Board Chairman Allan Greenspan also spoke out in favor of repealing most sections of Glass-Steagall, saying that such repeal would "respond effectively to the marked changes that have taken place in the financial marketplace both here and abroad."

As this chapter makes clear, "marked changes" would seem to understate the case.

Index